PARTNERING FOR FLUENCY

TOOLS FOR TEACHING LITERACY

Donna Ogle and Camille Blachowicz, Series Editors

This highly practical series includes two kinds of books: (1) grade-specific titles for first-time teachers or those teaching a particular grade for the first time; (2) books on key literacy topics that cut across all grades, such as integrated instruction, English language learning, and comprehension. Written by outstanding educators who know what works based on extensive classroom experience, each research-based volume features hands-on activities, reproducibles, and best practices for promoting student achievement.

TEACHING LITERACY IN SIXTH GRADE
Karen Wood and Maryann Mraz

TEACHING LITERACY IN KINDERGARTEN
Lea M. McGee and Lesley Mandel Morrow

INTEGRATING INSTRUCTION: LITERACY AND SCIENCE
Judy McKee and Donna Ogle

TEACHING LITERACY IN SECOND GRADE
Jeanne R. Paratore and Rachel L. McCormack

TEACHING LITERACY IN FIRST GRADE
Diane Lapp, James Flood, Kelly Moore, and Maria Nichols

PARTNERING FOR FLUENCY
Mary Kay Moskal and Camille Blachowicz

PARTNERING FOR
FLUENCY

Mary Kay Moskal
Camille Blachowicz

Series Editors' Note by Donna Ogle and Camille Blachowicz

THE GUILFORD PRESS
New York   London

© 2006 The Guilford Press
A Division of Guilford Publications, Inc.
72 Spring Street, New York, NY 10012
www.guilford.com

Printed in the United States of America

This book is printed on acid-free paper.

Last digit is print number: 9 8 7 6 5 4 3 2 1

Library of Congress Cataloging-in-Publication Data

Moskal, Mary Kay.
    Partnering for fluency / Mary Kay Moskal, Camille Blachowicz.
        p. cm. — (Tools for teaching literacy)
    Includes bibliographical refernces and index.
    ISBN-10 1-59385-264-9   ISBN-13 978-1-59385-264-1 (pbk.: alk. paper)
    ISBN-10 1-59385-265-7   ISBN-13 978-1-59385-265-8 (hardcover: alk. paper)
    1. Reading (Elementary)—United States.   2. Reading comprehension—
United States.   3. English language—Composition and exercises—Study and
teaching (Elementary)—United States.   I. Blachowicz, Camille.   II. Title.
III. Series.
    LB1573.M62 2006
    372.47—dc22
                                                                    2005032685

For Alexander

ABOUT THE AUTHORS

Mary Kay Moskal, EdD, is Associate Professor in the School of Education at Saint Mary's College of California. She is also codirector of the after-school literacy learning clinic at a local elementary school. Dr. Moskal has presented and published on the topic of fluency, both locally and nationally.

Camille Blachowicz, PhD, is Professor and Director of the Reading Program at National College of Education of National-Louis University. Dr. Blachowicz has published extensively on vocabulary, comprehension, and reading difficulties, and is a nationally known staff developer. She has also been named by the International Reading Association to the roster of Outstanding Reading Teacher Educators.

SERIES EDITORS' NOTE

This is an exciting time to be involved in literacy education. Across the United States, thoughtful practitioners and teacher educators are developing and fine-tuning their instructional practices to maximize learning opportunities for children. These cutting-edge practices deserve to be shared more broadly. Because of these changes, we have become aware of the need for a series of books for thoughtful practitioners who want a practical, research-based overview of current topics in literacy instruction. We also collaborate with staff developers and study group directors who want effective inservice materials that they can use with professionals and colleagues at many different levels that provide specific insights about literacy instruction. Thus the Tools for Teaching Literacy series was created.

This series is distinguished by having each volume written by outstanding educators who are noted for their knowledge and contributions to research, theory, and best practices in literacy education. They are also well-known staff developers who spend time in real classrooms working alongside teachers applying these insights. We think the series authors are unparalleled in these qualifications.

In this volume, master teacher and staff developer Mary Kay Moskal shares the experience that helped her develop her fluency partner program and, with her partner Camille Blachowicz, provides the background knowledge and research base teachers need to develop fluency partner programs in their own classrooms. The authors also share many other ideas for "putting a fluency spin" on instruction in the school curriculum. The classroom examples they have included in this volume can heighten a teacher's understanding of ways to develop fluency in meaningful and enjoyable ways.

DONNA OGLE
CAMILLE BLACHOWICZ

PREFACE

The title of this book is *Partnering for Fluency*—teachers working with students, and students working with other students as well as with parents and volunteers. It is fitting that the book's authors are two educational partners, Mary Kay Moskal and Camille Blachowicz. We have worked together in the area of fluency for the last 10 years, and we are excited to be able to share our experiences and learning with you in this book.

The purpose of this book is to share ideas that focus on:

➤ Understanding what fluent reading is and is not.

➤ Having a research base for your fluency work.

➤ Developing a literacy curriculum that covers fluency instruction for all children, including a partner model for fluency development.

➤ Knowing ways of assisting those students in greatest need of explicit fluency interventions.

➤ Providing resources for fluency instruction in the classroom and for individual professional development.

At one time, fluency was rarely included in reading programs. Educators today, however, clearly see the importance of fluency—and therefore it is now the focus of professional development and reading instruction. And no wonder! Reading fluency is highly correlated with many measures of reading competence. Fluent reading requires children to use good decoding skills and strategies, monitor their comprehension, and produce an expressive oral rendition of reading that demonstrates understanding. Nathan and Stanovich (1991) note that fluent reading is necessary for two things: (1) good comprehension, and (2) enjoyment. To put it another way, dysfluent readers usually have trouble understanding and draw little pleasure from reading. Bringing pleasure back into reading, especially for struggling readers, was one of the issues that led us to partnering for fluency.

Indeed, the special focus of our instructional approach is *partnering* for fluency. Practicing reading with a partner is a supportive way to develop fluency (Eldredge, 1990; Koskinen & Blum, 1986; Moskal, 2002). Especially for young children, the pleasure of working with a peer, teacher, or volunteer is often the key to effective fluency development.

Because we know that teachers are active and individual learners, this book is designed to be used by a range of educators in a variety of ways. The chapters explore the following themes:

➤ *Chapter 1. A Brief Look at Oral Reading Fluency.* This chapter covers basic concepts, vocabulary, and perspectives on fluency. This is a good place to start if you are new to the field of fluency education. It will help you to develop a vocabulary for fluency and build appropriate background knowledge to understand the subsequent chapters. In this chapter and throughout the book, Mary Kay interweaves first-person stories of her experiences in classrooms where fluency learning is taking place. These personal vignettes are intended to ground our observations in the "real-world" challenges that teachers encounter—and the solutions they have found—in making fluency instruction succeed for *all* their students.

➤ *Chapter 2. The Research Base.* We are all in the "age of accountability." Because we are called to have an evidence base for instruction, all chapters in this book cite relevant research. This chapter goes deeply into the research, questions, and controversies in the field. This is a good reference chapter for any work in fluency because it introduces you to the researchers, theoreticians, and practitioners who are making a difference in fluency instruction.

➤ *Chapter 3. Fluency Assessment.* Sensitive and relevant assessment is the teacher's best friend; it points the way to instructional goals and helps you to differentiate your instruction. This chapter discusses and gives examples of how fluency can be used as a screening assessment and how it can be assessed in different ways.

➤ *Chapter 4. Preparing for Fluency Instruction.* Good teachers are prepared teachers. Any time you start a new instructional process, preparation is key for smooth sailing. This chapter examines some of the issues related to materials, planning, and other processes that need to be considered before fluency instruction begins. How do you choose materials? What is the best way to proceed? This chapter will help you answer these questions.

➤ *Chapter 5. Fluency Lessons.* Once you are prepared, you have to select the best ways to meet the needs of your students. This chapter provides a survey of some of the most effective fluency lessons for students with different fluency needs. The chapter is organized to fit the ways in which most teachers organize their classes—instruction for whole groups and instruction for small groups; here we introduce some simple pair and partner activities.

➤ *Chapter 6. Student Partners for Fluency Development.* This is a key chapter of the book. Here we present our most novel ideas. The chapter reflects our recent research on how students working in pairs support each other's fluency development in what we call "a student self-managed repeated reading program." Detailed procedures and supporting explanations are provided along with useful tools for charting progress and growth.

➤ *Chapter 7. Volunteer Partners for Fluency Development.* Many classrooms and schools have volunteers, but few know how to use them for maximum effectiveness. This chapter shares specific procedures and ideas for a volunteer program that uses repeated readings to assist dysfluent readers. We provide detailed descriptions and charts used in our successful program, Everybody Reads.

➤ *Chapter 8. Resources for Fluency Instruction.* This chapter provides resources for your ongoing professional development in fluency work. It also includes detailed descriptions of commercial materials that can support fluency work in your classroom.

➤ *Chapter 9. Fluency as a Focus for Teacher Learning.* This final chapter focuses on fluency as a springboard for staff development. It is oriented toward reading specialists, coaches, and master teachers who want to use fluency work to reach a new level of curriculum and staff growth. The conclusion of this chapter is a synthesis and a call to action for you and your colleagues.

Join us as we share our passion for fluency with you. Become our partner in bringing the motivation and confidence that come from reading with fluency to your students, and you too will want to share the advantages of fluency instruction with others!

ACKNOWLEDGMENTS

Writing this book has been a humbling experience. So many people have lent their time and understanding. We wish to acknowledge the valuable support of the following people:

Candy Dawson Boyd, for providing valuable feedback;

The Everybody Reads participants, especially Peter Fisher, Connie Obrochta, Jennifer Massarelli, Susan Jones, Kathie Byers, Amy Sullivan, and Ellen Fogelberg, whose accomplishments remain a model for others to emulate;

Judy Mazur, who settles for nothing but exemplary literacy instruction in her classroom;

Paul Alejandrino, for his technical assistance;

Susan Pierce, Ayn Keneman, Cathy Conroy, Kathy Perez, and Susan Marston, for their endless encouragement; and

Joan, Chester, Michael, Mark, and Courtney, who graciously endured hours of writing during family vacations and holiday celebrations.

Heartfelt gratitude goes to Victor, Mary Kay's husband, and Alexander, her son, who have patiently lived with "the book," each honing new talents while she was busy writing. Victor became a brilliant cook and expert gardener while 6-year-old Alexander decided to become a writer, authoring numerous stories that he plans to send to *his* editor.

Camille thanks her family and colleagues for their usual patience and support.

Sincere thanks also to Christopher Jennison and Craig Thomas of The Guilford Press, for their always insightful comments and consistent encouragement.

CONTENTS

CHAPTER 1

A BRIEF LOOK AT ORAL READING FLUENCY

I sat in Judy's third-grade class listening to her students during guided reading one September morning. Judy had participated in a fluency workshop I led that summer and invited me to spend some time with her students. She wanted to focus on fluency instruction for her own professional growth that year, and I was there to observe and offer advice.

As I listened to the four groups of students, demonstrating various reading abilities, it was clear that the ablest readers needed little additional assistance with fluency. Their oral reading was smooth, graceful, and expressive, for the most part. The next group of students read well, too, but these readers were less expressive. They would, however, give a "punch" of enthusiasm to words or phrases to convey their interpretation of the reading.

The last two groups of students were not fluent. Students in the first group demonstrated repetition and frequent pauses. Their voices went up as they began a sentence and down as they completed the sentence, but the reading could not have been described as expressive. Students in the last group read in a word-by-word manner, with the children seemingly more interested in getting the word correct than in sounding fluent. Readers halted as they focused on each word individually, with little attention to phrasing or expression. It was difficult to listen to this monotonous reading.

After a while the children went to their morning recess, leaving Judy and me with some time to talk. We discussed a few methods and materials that she could incorporate into the curriculum to support the children. Judy agreed to try the suggestions and invited me back to observe. I continued to return to Judy's third-grade class at least once a week for that entire school year, sharing what I had learned about creating fluent readers while Judy sought to implement it. Judy and I became partners in introducing a fluency strand into the curriculum that would be appropriate for *all* the students in her class. We also formed a partnership with the children, and the children formed partnerships with each other. The parents even became partners in the goal of fluency.

In writing this book Camille and I are, in a way, partnering with you. Our goal is to introduce you to the variety of approaches and techniques available to integrate fluency instruction into your curriculum. To us, fluency is the gateway to mature reading, the bridge that leads to understanding.

AN OVERVIEW OF ORAL READING FLUENCY

Oral reading fluency—you know how it sounds because you have heard it; words read aloud effortlessly, accurately, and in an expressive manner. You have heard dysfluent reading, too; word calling in a choppy, detached manner, with long pauses, frequent repetitions, and little expression. Good readers seem fluent; less able readers seem dysfluent. Dysfluent readers can be found in almost every classroom at almost all grade levels and in high school.

Children learning how to read naturally sound choppy as they integrate decoding skills with a growing sight word vocabulary. With reading instruction and practice, some beginning readers easily transition from choppy word-by-word reading to natural-sounding reading. Others need guidance and support to develop fluency as they move into upper elementary and even middle school. Because this transition is not easy for all students, fluency, along with appropriate fluency assessment and instruction, is a viable area of concern in elementary classrooms.

So what exactly is fluency? Many teachers describe fluent reading as "sounding smooth." In addition, most teachers focus on rate as the sole indicator of a fluent reader. Although fluent reading *is* smooth, and rate is *one* indictor of fluent reading, fluency encompasses much more. Let's start by considering what reading fluency is and is not.

Some General Descriptions of Oral Reading Fluency

Oral reading fluency has been defined in numerous ways by various researchers, experts, and teachers. The word *fluency* comes from the Latin *fluens*, meaning to flow (Clark, 1995). Hence, oral reading fluency is generally described as flowing, smooth, and effortless. In order for a reading to be smooth and effortless, readers must be able to recognize and read words accurately, automatically, and quickly. In addition, the reading flows when prosodic elements are incorporated. Prosodic elements include appropriate phrasing, intonation, and expression, from which derive the rhythm and melody characteristic of a fluent reading.

There is still one more important feature of fluency: comprehension. Fluency and comprehension have an interesting relationship. Automatic word recognition skills allow a reader to recognize words fluently, freeing cognitive energy to focus on meaning. Yet this *automaticity* does not guarantee *understanding*. Have you ever had the experience of reading aloud in front of a group without having had any time to preread the material? I remember having to read somewhat difficult material aloud in college classes. My reading was fluent because I was skilled at word recognition, but I couldn't make sense of what I had just read—having focused all my energy on reading the words. I may have sounded fluent, but what's the point if I didn't understand? Similarly, English-language learners can become expert at decoding and word recognition, sound fluent while reading aloud, but lack the necessary vocabulary knowledge to understand what they read. Automaticity in word recognition is only one piece of the puzzle.

To complete the puzzle there must be a focus on constructing meaning from the text. It is the ongoing development of the text meaning that, in part, allows for the integration of prosody. As good readers recognize words and monitor their understanding, they seem to be able to integrate prosodic features into their oral reading. Good readers appear to be able to access prosodic cues from the text through their developing understanding and reading schema to produce a reading that is well phrased and expressive. So how are teachers able to teach all their students to be fluent readers who understand?

To support the development of fluent reading, it is necessary to understand dysfluency. Some definitions of oral reading fluency actually describe dysfluent reading or what fluency is *not*. Lipson and Lang (1991) identify four general types of dysfluent students: those who (1) are unable to recognize words automatically, (2) are unable to construct meaning from text because they rely too heavily on print and decoding, (3) fear reading and taking risks, and (4) haven't had extensive reading practice.

Let's take a look at each of these types of dysfluent readers. First, students who do not automatically recognize words take time to decode, causing the reading to sound choppy. Second, as in the example of reading difficult college material aloud, when readers spend most of their energy decoding, the ability to develop and retain meaning is compromised. With young readers especially, the lack of meaning can lead to inconsistent reading. Prosody is also threatened, and the reading may lack proper phrasing and intonation.

Some children are dysfluent because they do not want to make a mistake. In this situation students tend to pause to double check their accuracy. One student would add "Um" before each word he wasn't entirely sure he knew. The frequent pauses and insertion of "um" led to a dysfluent reading. With additional reading practice, this student built his confidence and improved his reading ability. Here we see how the simple lack of extensive reading practice can lead to dysfluency. Students need practice to progress, and practice will lead to fluency.

It is important to note that dysfluent oral reading is usually not the product of only one of the factors listed above but is rather a combination of these and possibly other factors. This combination of factors is one reason why teachers need to assess and address the development and unique profile of dysfluent readers through ongoing assessment and instruction. Understanding why a student is not fluent allows you to develop an optimal instructional plan for improvement.

As mentioned, many first and second graders make the transition from word calling to fluent reading with little effort. However, even with reading instruction, some children find the transition difficult and continue to read dysfluently into the upper elementary grades. Because fluent reading relies on a combination of factors, it is important to understand the basic elements of oral reading fluency, including (1) rate, (2) accuracy, and (3) prosody.

The Basic Elements of Oral Reading Fluency

Rate

A words-correct-per-minute (wcpm) reading rate is described as the number of words read correctly during 1 minute. Oral reading rates vary depending on the reader's grade level, text level, text genre, and reader's familiarity with the subject matter. Furthermore, narrative texts read for pleasure can usually be read faster than informational texts read to learn and remember.

Children in kindergarten and first grade normally read slower because they are beginners. Because they are just learning to read, teachers should not really worry about reading rates until the end of first grade (for some) or second grade (for most). Starting at second grade, oral reading rates increase for each grade level. Standards for oral reading rates are discussed in detail in Chapter 3.

The level of text difficulty can affect oral reading rates. If the text is too difficult, rates usually decrease, whereas if the text level is easy, rates usually increase. Rates can also decrease if, for example, the text is informational and the student reads to learn, or if the student has little knowledge of the subject matter. Think of reading a medical book because you are trying to learn how a simple surgery will be performed on your friend. As a novice, your reading rate is slow because of the medical terminology and the necessity to understand the procedure. In contrast, the surgeon reads the same passage with ease, at a high rate, and little effort toward understanding.

Accuracy

Accuracy refers to words read correctly in a reading. The larger the student's "bank" of high-frequency and sight words, the more accurate the reading. In addition, the better the student's ability to quickly and correctly decode words, the higher the accuracy. It is important to note that accurate word reading does not necessarily guarantee fluent reading.

Under the heading of accuracy, we would also like to mention semantics. Semantics refers to the process of making sense of read material—that is, creating meaning. Skillful readers expect what they read to make sense, monitor for understanding, and implement strategies when meaning breaks down. When an error is made in reading, it may affect meaning. For example:

> Correct sentence: A *house* is sitting on the hill.
>
> The child reads: A *hose* is sitting on the hill.

The skillful reader who has been monitoring for understanding will use strategies to self-correct the miscue when meaning breaks down. A *hose* sitting on a hill didn't seem to make sense within the context of the story, so the reader employed a rereading strategy and fixed the error.

On one hand, numerous self-corrections can affect the smoothness of a reading and therefore produce a dysfluent-sounding rendition of a passage. On the other hand, when errors and miscues are self-corrected, it is clear that the student is monitoring his or her understanding. If self-corrections are frequent, the student should reread at least a portion of the passage; such a rereading is usually more fluent.

Prosody

Prosodic reading, sometimes called expressive reading, requires appropriate phrasing, pausing, and use of intonation. Dowhower (1991), well known for her work with prosody, defines prosodic reading as "the ability to read in expressive rhythmic and melodic patterns" (p. 116). These rhythmic and melodic patterns occur naturally (i.e., they are required without formal instruction) in oral language. In talking, we add stress or accents to words and syllables, change our pitch to show the beginning and end of a sentence, and pause between words and sentences without conscious thought. When reading a written passage, in contrast, there are no markers, other than punctuation, to assist readers. In other words, written language includes few cues indicating where to pause for meaningful word chunks, how long to pause, when to change vocal intonation, or when to add emphasis to certain words. Oral reading is certainly not talking, but it should sound like talking, and without cues to help with prosody, some readers have a difficult time reading with expression. For many, prosodic reading involves modeling and practice.

The Connection between Oral Reading Fluency and Comprehension

Although fluency and comprehension are described as clearly connected, the way in which the two are connected is unclear. Research can be found to support the following three claims: (1) fluency supports comprehension, (2) comprehension supports fluency, or (3) both fluency and comprehension support each other.

To give you a sample of the research, we summarize what has been learned by those who have investigated fluency and comprehension. Allington (1983) explains that children who have had fluency instruction are better able to chunk words into meaningful phrases, thus improving comprehension. Nathan and Stanovich (1991) describe fluent readers as those whose word recognition skills are automatic; in turn, this automaticity is a contributing factor in comprehension. Lipson and Lang (1991) call fluent reading "an *instrument* for achieving comprehension" (p. 220; emphasis in original), and Bear (1991) claims that even with fluent reading, if there is no expression, there is no comprehension. A study done by Breznitz (1987) found that when reading rate increased, so too did text understanding. Dowhower (1987, 1989) and Herman (1985) found an increase in comprehension as a result of fluency development through repeated reading. And finally, Kuhn and Stahl (2000) note, from their review of studies related to fluency, that when fluency improved, for the most part comprehension improved as well.

Other studies go further, describing oral reading fluency as an indicator of basic reading ability. In other words, fluent readers tend to be abler readers. The reason seems to be found in fast word recognition. The ability to recognize words automatically allows for the employment of other complex reading processes, such as comprehension and higher-order thinking skills. The ability to read words tends to promote the meaning-making process, and understanding is a sign of a student's reading ability.

As mentioned before, though, this is not always the case—some struggling readers can read the words fluently but have difficulty understanding what they read. We see this particular problem frequently in the children recommended to our reading clinics. Some children know how reading should sound, and when they come to a word they don't know, they quickly substitute a different word so as not to lose the flow of the reading. Most of the time the substituted word begins with the same letter as the unknown word in the text, but it makes no sense in the context of the reading. Other children have learned their phonics skills well and can apply these skills in oral reading so that they sound fluent. However, when it comes to retelling the story and checking for understanding, the children have a difficult time. It's as though they don't realize that reading involves creating an understanding, not just word calling.

Fluency: An Integral Part of the Reading Curriculum

Until recently, teachers informally assessed fluency simply by listening to students read. "Read with expression!" was heard in many classrooms. Teachers knew fluent reading when they heard it, although it wasn't always clear how to support those students who were not expressive. For many years oral reading fluency activities were not promoted as an integral part of the well-balanced reading curriculum. Instruction in oral reading fluency was—and to some extent, still is—missing in many reading programs.

Readers need to integrate many literacy strategies as they read more difficult books and different genres. Practice helps, but some children have a hard time integrating all the skills necessary for a fluent reading. Even the best readers may have trouble reading expository genres fluently. It is for this reason that teachers should use instructional time to support students in fluency development at all grade levels. Most readers, fluent and dysfluent, benefit from classroom activities focusing on fluency.

Current use of basal reading series, professional publications, and staff development sessions assists classroom teachers to incorporate fluency instruction into the total reading program. And as a result of this greater emphasis on fluency instruction, increasing numbers of students are making progress in both fluency and reading, in general. It is clear that fluency instruction and practice are a vital part of a total reading program; in order to be fluent, good readers must orchestrate the fundamental processes of reading. In other words, fluent readers usually have good word recognition skills, are able to decode well, use strategies to assist with vocabulary and meaning, benefit from prior knowledge, and are able to monitor their understanding to allow for expressive reading (see Figure 1.1). Orchestrating or integrating these skills allows for fluency.

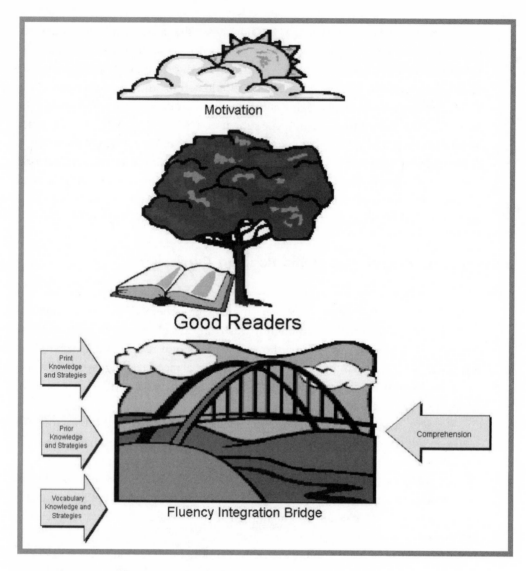

FIGURE 1.1. Good reader chart.

This integration is like learning to play tennis. The proper swing and footwork are practiced together in order to hit the ball where you want it to go. To play the game successfully, though, practice is necessary to integrate these two skills so that the player's attempt to return the ball becomes automatic.

When fluency instruction and practice are a regular part of the reading program, children are able to focus on this orchestration piece, whereby they integrate all their reading competencies into a fluent rendition of a passage. Furthermore, explicit fluency instruction may assist in closing the gap between competent readers and those who struggle (Blachowicz et al., 2006).

Judy invited me into her third-grade classroom to help her reconceptualize reading instruction to integrate the various aspects of fluency. We all worked together—Judy, the children, the parents, and I—as partners striving for fluent reading. By the end of the year, our work paid off: Not only were Judy's students fluent, but they also knew precisely what fluency was and what was necessary to achieve it.

LOOKING AHEAD

With this basic introduction to fluency, you have the background knowledge to help you begin to reconceptualize fluency instruction with your students. Chapter 2 provides a more extensive review of the research on fluency. If this chapter included enough research for you, then skip to Chapter 3.

THE RESEARCH BASE

AN OVERVIEW OF THE RESEARCH BASE

In my partnership with Judy, I shared books, research articles, and anecdotes to support her evolving understanding of fluency. Judy wanted to know everything. In fact, many times when I came to visit, Judy had a research article or book for me to read! Soon Judy was familiar with the research base from which fluency instruction was built; this learning allowed her to understand why she was implementing the various activities in her reading curriculum.

All of us are called upon to be accountable to students, parents, and administration for the education we provide. This accountability comes from the research that supports our teaching. This chapter, therefore, examines the research base for fluency, so that you can account for your instructional decisions.

As noted, fluent oral reading has a smooth, melodic rhythm that is free of frequent pauses and repetition. Fluency is an important component of good reading, and instruction in oral reading fluency is a necessary part of a balanced literacy curriculum. This chapter defines some important terminology and highlights studies relevant to oral reading fluency, repeated reading, and partnering for learning—all important parts of the classroom fluency process. The research for self-managed and collaborative learning (a topic discussed in Chapter 6) is included in this chapter.

11

A SHARED VOCABULARY

In Chapter 1 we began to develop a shared vocabulary for talking about fluency. It's important to have this shared vocabulary about the terms and concepts we are discussing, so let's delve into the terminology a little more deeply.

Oral Reading Fluency

Oral reading fluency is generally defined as smooth and effortless reading. For our purposes in this book, fluent oral reading is characterized by the three components described in Chapter 1: (1) appropriate reading rate, (2) accuracy, and (3) prosodic or expressive reading. Dysfluent reading is characterized by any or all of the following: (1) long pauses, (2) frequent repetitions, (3) substitution errors, (4) poor intonation, or (5) word-by-word reading. Each of these characteristics minimizes the flow of the reading or accounts for a failure in prosody.

Rasinski (2004) explains that "reading fluency refers to the reader's ability to develop control over surface-level text processing so that he or she can focus on understanding the deeper levels of meaning embedded in the text" (p. 46). In other words, fluent readers are able to focus their reading energy on understanding what they've read instead of focusing on decoding, word recognition, and prosody. Fluent readers have developed that orchestration of skills discussed in Chapter 1. Fluent readers are able to integrate, successfully and without conscious effort, prior knowledge, print knowledge, and vocabulary knowledge with well-developed comprehension skills. The combination of these skills not only builds understanding, but allows for a fluent oral reading.

Repeated Reading

Samuels (1979) is the founding father of the repeated reading process, decidedly one of the best strategies for fluency development. In the repeated reading process, a student reads an extended text passage of an appropriate level aloud while a teacher, clinician, or peer records miscues. After the first reading the child is coached to improve the next reading, then rereads the same passage, usually to work toward a predetermined fluency goal. In order for repeated reading to assist in fluency development, the coaching between the readings must be effective and highlight all aspects of fluency. In other words, repeated readings are most successful when rate, accuracy, and prosody are all emphasized over the course of the rereadings. In most repeated reading sessions, the reading is supported after the second reading and reread a third time.

After the first baseline reading, each rereading of the same passage is compared to previous readings to document improvement. Many times rate is a goal in repeated reading. However, even though rate is an essential component of fluency, speed reading should never be a focus. The focus should be on reading at the appropriate *pace*, otherwise children come to believe that reading faster is equal to reading better.

Passages of various reading levels can be selected for repeated readings, based on the type of partnership with the student. Clinicians and skilled teachers are able to use passages that would be considered difficult, or at a frustration level, to develop fluency, but this practice should be left to those who can provide intensive, structured support between readings. Instructional-level passages are appropriate when a child partners with a teacher or an adult volunteer; such passages provide a manageable amount of challenge for the student without being overwhelming. Finally, student partners are able to support each other when repeatedly reading independent-level passages. Passages at an independent level are relatively easy to read; the child should have few problems identifying the words and understanding the meaning of the passage.

Repeated reading is highly recommended by fluency experts. It is easy to implement and usually embraced by students because it is easy for them to hear themselves improve with each reading. Judy successfully used various forms of repeated reading during her literacy instruction. Throughout this book you will continue to encounter the strategy of repeated readings and various ways to implement it in the classroom.

Partnering for Fluency Development

I was observing a second-grade classroom in which student pairs were reading a passage repeatedly from their basal anthology. The partners had been assigned for the week, and Dorothy's partner was absent. Without the blink of an eye, Dorothy began the repeated reading process on her own, reading to herself. A classmate called, "You're doing that alone? Come and do it with us. We can have three partners." "No," said Dorothy, "I can handle it." So Dorothy read as if she had a partner. She even tried to take on the role of her partner by placing a Post-it arrow pointing to the words she had trouble reading, but she waited to mark the words until the end of the reading, and she couldn't remember which words they were. Dorothy went on to reread the passage two more times, playing the role of both the reader and the supportive partner, but seemed to be frustrated by the time she was finished. I asked her to talk to me about it. Dorothy said, "When someone's partner is not there, you can let the student work alone—but that might not be a good idea!" Dorothy went on to explain that she couldn't read and mark her miscues at the same time, and although she knew she was reading better by the second and third readings, she couldn't show it because she couldn't document her improvement.

And besides, it was boring working on reading without a partner! Dorothy explained, "We help each other *and* we have fun."

Dorothy's class frequently worked in pairs to tackle problems and complete assignments. She understood that she was part of a collaborative learning process in which she helped her partner, her partner helped her, and together they were successful. I found the partners in this class to be engaged, confident, supportive of each other, motivated, and interested. Most importantly, they were learning. In fact, I believe that they learned more than they could ever be "taught" while listening passively to a teacher or filling out worksheets.

This is just one example of the power of partnering. Maybe you have experienced partner work yourself. I used it when I was teaching young children, and I continue to use it with my college students because it works. Because both participants need to be engaged and accountable, the learning experience is usually enhanced. This sample of partnering is just to whet your appetite; you'll continue to discover more about partnering as you read further.

Self-Managed Learning

Student self-managed learning is frequently used to improve the academic skills of students in a variety of different curricula. "Self-management" is defined as the ability to control one's behavior in order to complete a task. Self-managed learning, therefore, is the ability to structure one's behavior not only to finish a task, but also to gain knowledge from the experience.

To assist students in using self-management techniques, a framework is provided along with modeling and guided practice. The guided practice exercises lead to independent practice in which the students manage themselves and learn at the same time. Self-managed learning is often used in conjunction with collaborative learning to enhance students' abilities to work efficiently and effectively as members of a group.

During part of the school year, Judy and I set up a system whereby the children managed a program focused on fluency improvement. Student partners worked together to collaborate and support each other's fluency development. Student self-management has been used successfully to promote fluency development. Chapter 6 describes student-managed fluency activities in more detail.

Collaborative Learning

"Collaborative learning," as it is used in elementary schools, is defined as groups or pairs of students working together toward a common goal. Our goal in this book is, of course, fluent reading. Positive interdependence is fostered when the activities used in collaborative learning are structured so that students share information, encourage each other, and support each other's efforts to achieve a goal. Students learning in a collaborative setting work as a highly effective team in the truest sense of the word. Each is bound to the other, so every member of the team reaches the goal. The success of the group relies heavily on the success of each member, whether it be a group of two (i.e., a pair) or a larger group.

Collaborative learning is characterized as a constructivist method of learning. Although the term is also used synonymously with "cooperative learning," there is a difference. In collaborative work groups are highly social, whereas in cooperative groups children can work with little social interaction. For example, cooperative group members are usually assigned a role they are to fulfill within the group. These roles might include the questioner, the summarizer, the time keeper, or the note taker. The roles allow the students to complete their task, and the task is completed as a result of the correct implementation of each role.

In contrast to cooperative learning, collaborative learning requires all members of the group to participate equally to complete a task. Predetermined roles are not assigned, and group members complete their task through spontaneous talk and moving in and out of roles related to the assignment. It can be noisy and impulsive, but the collaborative structure is closer to learning that occurs naturally, thereby encouraging self-efficacy. Just as students involved in cooperative groups are trained to implement their roles correctly, students involved in collaborative learning benefit from training in social strategies as well.

It is important for students to learn to work together effectively throughout the school year for collaborative learning to be successful. In Judy's class it was evident that her students frequently used collaborative group work to support learning. The practice they had already accrued, along with the support to problem solve, allowed them to easily transfer their skills as team members to work collaboratively on fluency activities.

RESEARCH ON ORAL READING FLUENCY

The Theoretical Foundations

The theory most frequently used to explain the ability to read fluently is LaBerge and Samuels' (1974) theory of automatic information processing. This theory suggests that students who are able to quickly and accurately decode and recognize words are then able to read aloud with rapidity, accuracy, and smoothness. Because words are read quickly and accurately, the reader can focus his or her attention on developing an understanding of meaning rather than on word recognition. A fluent oral rendition of a text is therefore a result of this combination of rapid word recognition and the ability to create meaning.

Samuels (1994) later adds that context has some bearing on the ability to read words quickly. For example, a passage with a large number of high-frequency and common words is read faster and with greater accuracy than a passage with difficult, unique, or content words. In our opinion this is important to remember when choosing reading materials for students. I (M.K.M.) remember my first experience as a student at the university reading an article about literacy assessment in *Reading Research Quarterly*. I had the prior knowledge to assist me in understanding, but the number of unfamiliar words unique to assessment (I still remember encountering the word *psychometric*) made the reading slowgoing. I was unable to read the article fluently.

A different focus central to fluent oral reading is the role of prosody. In written language there are limited prosodic cues to aid a reader in determining appropriate intonation, phrasing, and pausing, also called "juncture." In other words, written language doesn't mark where to chunk words into meaningful mini-phrases, how long to pause between mini-phrases, when to change the intonation or pitch of one's voice, or when to add emphasis or stress to certain words or syllables (Dowhower, 1986, 1987; Schreiber, 1980).

To demonstrate, let's look at the sentence:

In order to be fluent, readers need to chunk words into meaningful phrases.

The obvious cues in this sentence include a comma and a period. What should a reader know, based on these cues? Well, there should be a pause at the comma and an even longer pause after the period, but these are the only cues that are marked. Readers must therefore determine everything else on their own! First, declarative sentences begin with a rising pattern in the voice and end with a falling pattern. Next, the sentence begins with a phrase that contains its own rise and fall pattern and can be segmented into two chunks: (1) *in order* and (2) *to be fluent*. When reading this phrase aloud, a reader might include a slight pause after the word *order* to indicate the end of the first of the two "chunks" and a stress on the first syllable of flú·ent before lowering the pitch of the voice to cue the end of the phrase. After a slightly longer pause to represent the comma, the remainder of the sentence might be chunked in this manner with the slash marks denoting a slight pause:

readers need / to chunk words / into meaningful phrases.

A stress might be placed on the words *chunk* and *meaningful* to convey their importance within the sentence as a whole.

When you read the sentence to yourself, you may have interpreted the prosodic cues differently—and that's fine. The point is that some children don't realize that they need to account for these meaningful yet invisible elements in order to be fluent. It is beneficial for most readers to participate in activities that provide support in extracting prosodic information from the text, chunking mini-phrases, and inserting pitch, stress, and juncture.

Fluency Instruction Begins in Second Grade

Various researchers have investigated when the time is right in the reading development of children to begin explicit instruction in fluency. Allington (1983) believes it is the child who can decode but lacks the ability to phrase correctly and reads without expression who will benefit the most from fluency instruction. Bear (1991) agrees, adding that students should have a good understanding of basic spelling—its regular patterns, letter sequences, and irregularities—before fluency instruction would be beneficial. Strecker, Roser, and Martinez (1998) describe the reader's shift from attending to words and decoding strategies to meaning as the prime time for fluency development. Because these descriptions point to the reading development of typical second graders, it is usually wise to begin fluency instruction in second grade. Of course, there will be a wide variety of reading abilities within any group of students, so some children may be ready for fluency instruction during the second half of first grade.

All students can benefit from fluency instruction, but which students need the most support? Some research suggests that students who are unable to chunk words into meaningful phrases or continue to read word by word are in need of explicit fluency instruction. Lipson and Lang (1991) propose a different way of thinking about students who need specific fluency instruction. They recommend asking the questions, "What can this child read fluently?" and "Does the range of situations require expanding?" (p. 225). They suggest that teachers find materials that the student can read fluently, decide if these materials are at an appropriate level for the child and grade level, and determine if the child should be reading more difficult materials fluently.

The format suggested by Lipson and Lang is put into practice in our reading clinics. During the initial assessment battery of each child above first grade, the clinicians obtain fluency samples from a wide variety of reading levels with both narrative and expository passages. With specific information on rate, accuracy, smoothness, phrasing, and prosody, the clinicians can determine what the student can read fluently and where they need to focus their efforts so that the student can receive optimal fluency instruction.

RESEARCH ON REPEATED READING

The Theoretical Foundations

The theoretical rationale for using repeated reading in developing fluency is the same theory that supports oral reading fluency, in general. In the theory of automatic information processing, developed by LaBerge and Samuels (1974), readers need to attend to comprehension to create meaning from the words. As a result readers must possess a high degree of automaticity in decoding and word recognition so that their energy can be focused on understanding what is being read. It is the repetition in reading a passage that affords students the ability to read with less attention at the word level, thus freeing up attention for developing meaning. Samuels (1979) compares repeated reading with the training that is necessary for success in sports and music. He writes, "Decoding [of a musical score] must be done automatically so that the mind of the musician is free to play the score with emotion and feeling" (p. 407). So, too, is the case in repeated reading, where each subsequent reading frees the mind further for improved word reading, prosody, and understanding.

There is one caveat, though. Teachers, wanting students to acquire automatic decoding skills, should not believe that providing more phonics and decoding lessons, especially when taught in isolation, will lead to fluency. Automatic word recognition does not produce fluency, but it does help in reading fluently.

A different theoretical rationale is also suggested for the use of repeated reading in fluency development. In rereading, children are able to pick up those unmarked prosodic cues and become capable of reading with appropriate phrasing and expression. Dowhower (1986) elegantly describes the way children use repeated reading to move toward prosodic reading: "RR [repeated reading] helps the reader learn that although the words are printed in one-by-one fashion on a page, a reader must learn to process them in units of thought, much as he talks" (p. 10). This is done "through successive approximations that gradually allow children to chunk text into meaningful phrases until the rhythm and melody sound like talking" (Dowhower, 1987, p. 404). In other words, fluent reading implies a move past just reading words; fluent reading indicates an interpretation of the text that allows for reading with expression. The fluent reader shows understanding by reading with an expressive interpretation.

Repeated Reading as an Effective Tool for Fluency Development

In repeated reading, students read, then reread, a passage for either a predetermined amount of times or to reach a fluency goal. We'd like to offer two powerful reasons for using repeated reading for fluency development. First, this process clearly impacts fluency. Rasinski (1989) cites repeated reading as a method proven to increase rate and accuracy. By the first rereading of a passage, rate tends to increase and miscues tend to decrease. Second, repeated reading affects prosody. Dowhower (1987) noted a significant improvement in the ability of second graders to read in meaningful phrases with the use of repeated readings. Other researchers stress the reader's increased ability to pick up on prosodic cues with each rereading.

Repeated Reading Considerations

A number of repeated reading methods are used for fluency development. In general, the repeated reading strategy entails the rereading of a short passage two or three times in one session. For subsequent repeated reading sessions, the same or a different passage is chosen, and the rereading procedure is followed again. A brief description of general considerations regarding the implementation of repeated reading is provided next.

Repeated Reading with Adult–Student Partnering

Repeated reading is most effective when students partner with an adult or a more capable student who can provide appropriate and immediate feedback to the reader between readings. With the additional support, the readings that follow tend to improve as rate increases, miscues decrease, and prosody develops. An added bonus is that with repeated readings, understanding deepens as well.

Repeated Reading with Student–Student Partnering

One method of repeated reading used with student partners is called "paired repeated reading." Paired repeated reading usually involves (1) students selecting their own reading materials, (2) both partners taking turns rereading the chosen passage, and (3) both partners evaluating their own and their partner's read-aloud for fluency elements. Paired repeated reading is easy to use and manage, engaging for the students, and especially successful for below-average readers. In addition, if the repeated reading is coupled with positive feedback from the listening partner between the readings, the benefits tend to increase.

Text Selection for Repeated Reading

Successful fluency development requires students to read passages of 50–300 words in length. To make this easier, we suggest that the students choose a passage and count the lines, figuring an approximate average of 10 words per line. You will need to check your students' choices to see if this system works with the books available for your grade level.

There is evidence that students can improve fluency by using materials at all reading levels: independent, instructional, and frustration (Kuhn & Stahl, 2000). Dowhower (1989) and Blachowicz et al. (2000) suggest that passages read at an 85% or better accuracy rate (that means no more than 15 errors in 100 running words of text) on the first reading would also be appropriate for fluency work with an adult partner. Easy materials (no more than five errors in 100 running words of text) allow readers to feel successful because they can decode with few errors, thus allowing effort to be put into prosody and understanding. This easy or independent level is appropriate for student-led or paired repeated readings.

Instructional-level texts offer a degree of challenge that helps to maintain the student's motivation without eliciting frustration. Kuhn and Stahl (2000) report that the support provided between the readings is the core element of the success found with instructional-level passages. With intense support, frustration-level materials can also be used successfully.

At the reading clinics, we have seen students improve fluency with texts that were much too difficult. Such improvement requires a strong, intuitive coach and an extremely motivated student. For example, Ryan, a fifth-grade student, was assessed to be reading at a first-grade level. Although he loved baseball, he did not want to read the cartoon versions of baseball stories written at a level with which he could find success. The reading coach presented Ryan with a number different baseball books so that he could choose what he wanted to read. His choices included picture books, chapter books, and informational texts—all on the subject of baseball. Ryan chose *The World of Baseball* (Buckley, 2003). His reading coach commented:

> "I think he likes the look of the book because it is similar to what his class-mates might choose. It's definitely too hard for him, but he wants to read it. I mean, he's so motivated to read it! The great thing about this book, though, is that there are small pictures and captions in the margins where the print is the just about the same size as the rest of the text. We usually start with these because they are short and with just one rereading he sounds fluent. This builds his confidence and he is ready to read the rest!"

Ryan's reading coach used different strategies (discussed later in this book) to support his fluency, and in time he not only finished the baseball book, but he continued to reread it, selecting this book over recess when he was early for a tutoring session!

STUDENT SELF-MANAGED LEARNING

Repeated reading is a versatile strategy that has been used in classrooms to develop fluency in a variety of ways. One way involves student pairs in which each student works as a clinician for the other. This procedure, involving student self-management and repeated reading activities, is described in Chapter 6. The research base for student self-managed learning is presented here.

The Theoretical Foundations

Specific theoretical foundations for self-managed learning are difficult to pinpoint. Literature on the various components of "self" and the particular development of the different self systems is not integrated into one universal understanding or theoretical foundation. This means that separate methods or approaches of different self systems include relatively dissimilar foundations.

John Dewey's (1916/1944; Perkinson, 1976) writings seem to fit particularly well into a foundation for self-managed learning. As Dewey explained his view, education is, and should be, a process of actively engaging students in the *construction* of learning. Children should not just be told what they must learn, as if the teacher were transferring knowledge into empty heads! Children should become motivated to learn information presented at school, begin to explore and manipulate materials in that area, and learn by noticing that which they had not noticed before. In other words, children need to be actively involved in inquiry and discovery in an area of study for optimal learning. It is a circular process: Children grow through learning, and growing is necessary for further growth and learning. In self-managed learning situations, initiative, independence, and resourcefulness are developed while motivation and a love of learning are nurtured. Dewey saw optimal learning as directed by oneself to promote further learning, a work ethic, and motivation.

Much of Dewey's theory has been confirmed in recent research conducted on the human brain. Caine and Caine (1991) explain that within the brain there is an innate need to make sense of the world, a drive to learn or make meaning. In developing the self, emotions and challenges come into play as children become empowered by doing and learning on their own. Because children who are involved in self-managed learning are able to learn without feeling vulnerable, they feel an intrinsic motivation that elevates their passion for learning and their feelings of self-esteem.

Why Self-Managed Learning?

When students are actively involved in the implementation of their own education through self-management techniques, the entire learning experience is brought to a heightened intensity as they assume responsibility for their scholarship and behavior. They see the value of the learning process as they become aware of the management and control necessary for achieving their learning goals.

While teacher effort is spent modeling self-managed learning processes and supplying necessary resources, student effort is spent in pursuing and consciously trying to achieve their learning goals. This active, constructive education is what Dewey described as cultivating intrinsic motivation and thus interest and understanding. In supporting learning through self-managed activities, students realize the purpose in reading and learning, which in turn helps them develop a positive sense of self.

Let's take the example of Pamela, a fourth-grade, below-average reader who aspired to read better. In fact, Pamela was *determined* to read better; she wanted to be able to read her town's newspaper articles aloud to her grandmother, who was ill. Pamela's teacher paired her up with Sandra, a fifth grader who had low self-esteem, for 10 minutes a day before the bell rang in the morning. The teacher trained the two girls together, using fluency-building methods, and then the girls worked on their own in the school's library. Both girls felt a responsibility: Pamela, to learn to read fluently, and Sandra, to help Pamela achieve this goal. Both girls behaved in a very professional manner, understanding that they had a short amount of time in which to complete their task. Both girls felt an intrinsic motivation, especially as the lessons continued, because Pamela was getting noticeably better, and Sandra knew she was the reason. In addition both girls improved their reading abilities, and they did it on their own, by managing a 10-minute block of time for fluency work.

The Connection between Self-Managed Learning and Motivation

Reading motivation includes beliefs children have about themselves and their abilities. A motivated reader will develop a sense of self-efficacy and high expectations for success. For example, I watched a first grader try to read *Cook-A-Doodle-Doo!* (Stevens & Crummel, 1999), a picture book about the Little Red Hen's Great Grandson and his attempt at making strawberry shortcake. Although the reading was challenging, the child did not appear to feel threatened, because he was motivated and believed he had the ability to read it to himself. He persisted through the "hard words" and when he got to the end, he not only beamed but went back to the beginning, called a friend over to join him, and started all over again.

Self-managed learning can enhance this kind of motivation because children working in self-managed learning situations usually develop a sense of high expectations and self-efficacy. Children are able to work toward a learning goal that they value—a goal such as learning to read well. The most powerful motivation comes from what the individual considers important, as shown by the first grader who valued the ability to read that book. In an atmosphere of high challenge (the challenge was to read that picture book) and low risk (there were no consequences if he found he couldn't read it), children are able to strive toward their goals. Self-managed learning develops motivated, involved children who assume success.

Motivation is connected to success, and the student self-managed repeated reading process (described in Chapter 6) is, in most instances, able to intensify motivation because the results almost always demonstrate success upon completion of the process. This process appears to enhance or create a sense of self-efficacy, as students learn to *expect* improvement with each repeated reading procedure. Recursively, self-efficacy enhances intrinsic motivation because the reinforcement of succeeding and improving leads students to want to continue the process for the sole sake of learning and improving. It's a wonderful cycle that leads to high self-esteem and improved fluency.

LEARNING IN COLLABORATIVE PAIRS

Another way to support a positive sense of self is through collaborative learning. Collaborative groups can be used for activities that involve problem solving, practice, and review of learning materials. It is a child-centered method of instruction found to be effective with students of varying academic abilities. There is a great deal of social interaction in collaborative learning that allows students to take responsibility for their own learning as well as the learning of others in the partnership; most students see it as learning that is fun. Children simply enjoy activities in which they can both learn with others and be actively involved. This active learning and participation enhance self-efficacy, which in turn increases student success.

Learning collaboratively is vitally important to the self-managed learning process. Whether in small groups or in pairs, collaborative work seems to help children become excited about the task in which they are involved and want to learn more. In their study of collaborative partners, Koskinen and Blum (1986) observed children working in pairs on repeated reading for fluency development. They note that "students enjoy working together and derive considerable pleasure and self-confidence" (p. 74). Although pleasure and confidence are important, there are other reasons why working in collaborative groups or pairs benefits the students. As noted, Dewey (1916/1944) pointed out the benefits of learning that occurs in a social environment. He believed that it is the cognitive and emotional aspects of learning in a social environment that allow for true education. Working together promotes an emotional connection to other students and the learning, which in turn enhances motivation and a desire to learn more and more.

Dysfluent Partners in Collaborative Pairs

In Chapter 6, a student-centered repeated reading activity is described in detail. This activity is unique because it is the first to pair equally dysfluent partners in an effort to help each other become more fluent. Other fluency partnering models suggest that one of the partners be a more capable reader, but Rogoff (1990) and Forman and Cazden (1994) embrace the model wherein the partners are at the same level of inability, inexperience, or understanding.

Generally in this model, which is sometimes described as "novice peer partnering," the paired children serve as resources for each other through their talk while completing the task on which they are working. For example, one child assumes the role of a teacher observing, assisting, and correcting while the other works on the task. The child/teacher-partner is able to provide the kind of assistance that has been described as scaffolding, supporting the partner in a way that assures achievement. Moreover, student partners seem to be able to interchange their teacher-partner/student-partner roles easily, offering information, giving and following directions, and asking questions—all within the same context.

Further evidence of the efficacy of novice peer partnering comes from Piaget (Rogoff, 1990), who explained that when student pairs approach a task as equals, they are able to restructure their thinking based on the other's point of view and logic. This same kind of exchange does not occur with an adult–student pair because the adult holds the balance of power. In addition, Piaget believed that children treat situations in a different way when they, not the adult, are in charge (Rogoff, 1990). Children in charge tend to be more playful and exploratory in their learning. When an adult is one of the partners, the work is more direct and on task.

A FINAL WORD

We are continually called to explicate a research base for our school practices. For those of us interested in fluency, the research on oral reading fluency, repeated readings, self-managed learning, and collaborative classroom work are all important to both understanding the issues surrounding fluency and to structuring appropriate fluency instruction. Now that you understand the foundations of fluency and the other subjects discussed in this book, let's move to our next concern, the assessment of fluency.

CHAPTER 3

FLUENCY ASSESSMENT

ecause the finest classroom instruction comes from an analysis of carefully designed assessments, Judy began the school year with assessment. As is the case for many subject areas, fluency assessment is the foundation for individualizing optimal instruction for each child. Judy wanted to be able to track the development of her students' fluency over the course of the school year. She wanted baseline information in the fall, informal assessments she could use during instruction, and an assessment battery she could implement three times a year to document growth and compare students to each other. All this information would help her plan instruction throughout the year for all her students, focus on those who needed the most support, and share strengths and challenges with parents.

Fluency assessments are developed to provide information for instruction and to document growth, but before discussing fluency assessment options, it is important to gain familiarity with the general ways of measuring fluency for instruction and assessment. These sources provide the data teachers can use to compare students' performances with established baseline rates and plan instruction accordingly. The sources include rate, accuracy, and fluency scales. The selection of appropriate passages for fluency assessment is also important.

FLUENCY MEASUREMENT FOR INSTRUCTION AND ASSESSMENT

Rate

Obtaining a words-correct-per-minute (wcpm) rate continues to be the most common way to assess oral reading fluency. Calculating this rate is also thought to be the most effective assessment of fluency, although just looking at the reading rate does not take the quality of reading into account. Because the measurement of a words-correct-per-minute rate is sensitive to small increments of change, it is, however, excellent for documenting growth over time. For example, Anna, a struggling fourth grader, was reading *Tales of a Fourth Grade Nothing* (Blume, 1991). She read a passage three times over three sessions. Her reading rates are listed in Table 3.1. Anna has clearly improved her words-correct-per-minute rate over the nine readings, and also over the course of the first reading in each session. But is she reading at an appropriate rate for a fourth grader?

Anna's words-correct-per-minute rate should also be compared to a standard. This standard allows teachers to make decisions for instruction based on grade-level norms. Blachowicz, Sullivan, and Cieply (2001) recommend the guidelines for oral reading rates listed in Table 3.2. These rate guidelines are comparable to those suggested by other experts.

Anna read a passage from the *Tales of a Fourth Grade Nothing* at a rate of 118 words correct per minute after the ninth reading of the passage. She finally reached the grade-level standard. Because her teacher's goal was to continue rereading a passage until Anna reached the grade-level rate range, it was time to move onto another passage for repeated reading. But how did the rereading affect Anna's reading accuracy?

Accuracy

Accurate reading is reading that has few or no errors. Materials used for fluency assessment and instruction should be read at an 85% or better accuracy rate for a first reading of the selection. In other words, students work with texts that are not too difficult. If student peers are working on improving their fluency without the assistance of a more capable reader,

TABLE 3.1. Anna's Oral Reading Fluency Rates

Session	First reading	Second reading	Third reading
1	79 wcpm	85 wcpm	89 wcpm
2	80 wcpm	87 wcpm	90 wcpm
3	93 wcpm	96 wcpm	118 wcpm

TABLE 3.2. Guidelines for Average Oral Reading Fluency Rates

Grade level	Oral reading rate range
1	30–70
2	60–90
3	80–120
4	100–120
5	120–150

Note. From Blachowicz, Sullivan, and Cieply (2001). Copyright 2001 by Taylor & Francis, Inc. Reprinted by permission.

then material read should be read at a 95% or better accuracy rate, although students have been successful working independently with materials at a 93% accuracy rate (Moskal, 2002).

Because Anna's first reading was 96% accurate, with only five errors, her teacher knew the material was not too hard for her. By the second session, Anna's third rereading improved to 99% accuracy, and she achieved 100% accuracy on the last rereading. Although accuracy and rate offer good information, there is little to describe the way Anna's reading sounded. To obtain information on prosody, her teacher turned to a fluency scale.

Fluency Scales

Teachers who assess fluency by obtaining only a words-correct-per-minute rate are not getting a complete picture of their student's fluency. Rate and accuracy allow teachers to assess the quantitative aspects of fluency, but fluency scales assess the qualitative aspects that encompass how the reading sounds.

A few scales are available for teachers to use. One is the Integrated Reading Performance Record developed and used by the National Assessment of Educational Progress (NAEP; Pinnell et al., 1995; see Table 3.3). This four-level scale is widely used by researchers and teachers, but a common critique is that the scale does not address the qualitative features of fluency consistently within each of the levels (Herman, 1985). The scale is very useful in documenting growth, but often not practical for planning specific fluency instruction.

Another popular scale, the Multidimensional Fluency Scale, was developed by Zutell and Rasinski (1991) and then updated by Rasinski in 2004 (see Table 3.4). This scale is divided into the categories of expression and volume, phrasing, smoothness, and pace—each with four levels of competence. Teachers who use this scale are able to pinpoint specific fluency needs, thereby streamlining their instruction for individuals and small groups.

To see how these two scales work, let's consider Kashie, who is in fifth grade and has been in the United States for 4 years. Kashie had learned how to decode

TABLE 3.3. NAEP's Integrated Reading Performance Record

Level 4   Reads primarily in larger, meaningful phrase groups. Although some regressions, repetitions, and deviations from the text may be present, these do not appear to detract from the overall structure of the story. Preservation of the author's syntax is consistent. Some or most of the story is read with expressive interpretation.

Level 3   Read primarily in three- or four-word phrase groups. Some smaller groupings may be present. However, the majority of phrasing seems appropriate and preserves the syntax of the author. Little or no expressive interpretation is present.

Level 2   Reads primarily in two-word phrases with some three- or four-word groupings. Some word-by-word reading may be present. Word groupings may seem awkward and unrelated to larger context of sentence or passage.

Level 1   Reads primarily word-by-word. Occasionally two-word or three-word phrases may occur, but these are infrequent and/or they do not preserve meaningful syntax.

Note. From Pinnell et al. (1995, p. 15).

well but struggled sometimes with meaning. She could pronounce many words correctly, but would add stress to words and within sentences improperly, especially if what she was reading was unfamiliar. Because she was still learning about English and U.S. culture, she was confused by many phrases and vocabulary. For example, Kashie was stunned when she read that a character said, "Catch you later" and ate chocolate *mousse.* This confusion was often displayed in dysfluent reading.

Kashie's fluency was assessed three times over the course of the school year, using the NAEP scale on the reading of a fifth-grade benchmark passage. In September she scored a level 2, in January a level 3, and in June a level 4. It was easy to use the NAEP scale to validate her progress over the course of the year. The NAEP scale was also used to assess five consecutive reading sessions midyear during guided reading. Kashie's fluency scores on the NAEP scale ranged between levels 2 and 4 for each of the five readings. Sometimes her phrasing was appropriate but her reading sounded choppy as she tried to read for understanding. Many times she read with the expression described in level 4, but the rest of her reading could not be assessed as a level 4. At other times her intonation was wrong, and her teacher would note this incorrectness next to her fluency-level score because she felt the scale didn't explain it well enough.

TABLE 3.4. Multidimensional Fluency Scale

Expression and volume

1   Reads words as if simply to get them out. Little sense of trying to make text sound like natural language. Tends to read in a quiet voice.

2   Begins to use voice to make text sound like natural language in some areas of the text but not in others. Focus remains largely on pronouncing the words. Still reads in a quiet voice.

3   Makes text sound like natural language through the better part of the passage. Occasionally slips into expressionless reading. Voice volume is generally appropriate throughout the text.

4   Reads with good expression and enthusiasm throughout the text. Varies expression and volume to match his or her interpretation of the passage.

Phrasing

1   Monotonic with little sense of phrase boundaries, frequent word-by-word reading.

2   Frequent two- and three-word phrases giving the impression of choppy reading; improper stress and intonation that fail to mark ends of sentence and clauses.

3   Mixture of run-ons, mid-sentence pauses for breath, and possibly some choppiness; reasonable stress/intonation.

4   Generally well phrased, mostly in clause and sentence units, with adequate attention to expression.

Smoothness

1   Frequent extended pauses, hesitations, false starts, sound-outs, repetitions, and/or multiple attempts.

2   Several "rough spots" in text where extended pauses, hesitations, etc., are more frequent and disruptive.

3   Occasional breaks in smoothness caused by difficulties with specific words and/or structures.

4   Generally smooth reading with some breaks, but word and structure difficulties are resolved quickly, usually through self-correction.

Pace (during sections of minimal disruption)

1   Slow and laborious.

2   Moderately slow.

3   Uneven mixture of fast and slow reading.

4   Consistently conversational.

Note. From Rasinski (2004, p. 49). Copyright 2004 by Timothy Rasinski. Reprinted by permission.

The Multidimensional Fluency Scale, on the other hand, showed a pattern that her teacher could use to plan for fluency development. Kashie always scored a 4 on expression and volume; she had good volume and usually read the entire passage with expression and enthusiasm. Kashie scored 2's and 3's on phrasing due to intonation difficulties related to learning English. She consistently scored a 3 on smoothness, revealing occasional problems with words and structures, and a 4 on pace, reflecting a conversational pace. Kashie's teacher used the Multidimensional Fluency Scale scores to document the difficulty she had with phrasing, especially intonation. With this information she was able to focus Kashie's instructional plan as well as share the assessment with her parents.

There is one final scale developed for those students who equate fluent reading with speed reading. Some students respond to explicit fluency instruction by reading too fast and ending up dysfluent. Both teachers and students can use the Excessive Speed Reading scale (ESR) found in Table 3.5 (Moskal, 2002).

Zac was a fairly fluent reader, but despite his teacher's lessons on the components of fluency, Zac decided that fast reading was good reading. Zac was coached to slow down and use the right pace, but to him fast *was* the right pace. He believed that if he finished his reading before anyone else, then he was the best. His teacher introduced the Excessive Speed Reading (ESR) scale to his group during a guided reading lesson. Student pairs described levels A, B, and C to each other and the teacher explained levels D and E. The children were then assigned the task of rewriting the scale using words that were easier to understand. Not only did Zac begin reading at the right pace, but the children introduced their rewritten scale to the class, posted it in the room, and were heard referring their classmates to it when they thought a reading was too fast during silent sustained reading!

Teachers who have used NAEP's Integrated Reading Performance Record, the Multidimensional Fluency Scale, and the ESR scale have reported that initially they had to reread the scales often when assessing fluent reading, but in a short period of time and with frequent use they became sufficiently familiar that they rarely needed to

---

TABLE 3.5. Excessive Speed Reading Scale

A   The reading sounds too fast.

B   The reading is characterized by mumbling and the swallowing of words.

C   There is little expression.

D   Reading is disrupted by pauses to stop and breathe.

E   Phrase boundaries are compromised.

Note. The rating does not reflect a hierarchical order. From Moskal (2002, p. 61). Reprinted by permission of the author.

refer to them. One teacher found it easiest to keep the scale he used on a laminated sheet tucked in his record book so that he could review it, when needed.

Passage Selection

Students should be reading connected text of 50–300 words in length for both assessment and instruction. When using text for fluency, leveled passages may be used for different situations. Easy materials allow readers to feel successful because they are able to decode effortlessly and put their effort into prosodic reading and comprehension. Instructional-level materials present more of a challenge, and materials at the frustration level are the most difficult. More information on passage selection for instruction follows in Chapter 4; here we focus on passage selection for assessment.

It is important to consider reading level along with rate and accuracy levels when documenting the results of an assessment. For example, Zac's independent reading level was fourth grade, instructional was fifth/sixth grade, and frustration was seventh grade. During the end-of-the-year assessments in sixth grade he read aloud 173 words correct per minute on a fourth-grade passage, 153 words correct per minute on the fifth-grade passage, 142 words correct per minute on the sixth-grade passage, and 118 words correct per minute on the seventh-grade passage. Zac's fluency rate changed noticeably based on the passage selected for assessment. At the sixth-grade level, Zac's reading was slow, but he was able to read at the appropriate rate on a fifth-grade passage. This pattern could be interpreted in two ways: (1) Zac's fluency rate is below average on sixth-grade-level reading materials, or (2) Zac's fluency rate is average on reading materials 1 year below grade level.

The fluency sources of rate, accuracy, fluency scales, and passage selection lay the foundation for the information in the next section on fluency assessments.

ASSESSMENT TOOLS

Classroom Fluency Snapshots

A simple but useful classroom assessment tool is the classroom fluency snapshot (CFS). Blachowicz et al. (2001) describe this assessment tool as one that is quick and easy to administer and that produces a baseline with which to compare all students in one classroom. It is popular with teachers because it allows them to examine the fluency status of their students along a continuum and document changes, or lack thereof, throughout the school year (see Table 3.6).

TABLE 3.6. Second-Grade Classroom Fluency Snapshot

wcpm range	Student, wcpm rate	wcpm range	Student, wcpm rate
175	Courtney, 172	85	
170		80	
165		75	Emie, 75
160		70	
155		65	Becky, 64
150		60	
145	Alex, 144	55	Matt, 56
140		50	Alli, 51
			Katie, 52
135	Matty, 133		
130		45	
125	Shelly, 121	40	
120	April, 118	35	
	Tom, 119	30	Hector, 32
115	Joe, 112	25	
110		20	Michael, 23
			Suzie, 20
105	DeAndre, 104	15	Violet, 14
100		10	
95	Dalton, 94	05	
	Heather, 95		
90	Keith, 93		
	Cassie, 91		

Note. CFS administered in January. The average second-grade words-correct-per-minute range is 60–90.

The procedure includes a brief 3- to 5-minute session with each student. All students read the same passage for 1 minute while the teacher listens and records miscues. A teacher might begin the assessment by saying, "I would like you to read to me for about a minute. I am going to watch the time to be sure it is not much longer than a minute. I have a copy of the same passage, and I'm going to mark how you read. This will help me understand how you think about reading, so I can help you to learn more and become a better reader."

Most teachers select a benchmark passage for the CFS and use that same passage in September, January, and June. A benchmark passage would be one that a typical student at that grade level might read midway through the school year. This means at any point in the school year the passage might be too easy or too hard for some students. Even so, it is important to use the same passage throughout the year to allow for consistency and comparison. Teachers have included struggling readers in the CFS assessment not only to assess where they would fall along the classroom continuum, but also to record growth, or lack thereof.

Some students may not be ready for this assessment. For example, the CFS is not recommended for most first graders until the end of the school year because many first graders do not have solid decoding skills until the spring, and some are still novices at combining word reading and understanding in the same reading. Likewise, some second graders may not be reading in the fall, and students for whom English is a second language may not have acquired the needed proficiency. These children would participate in the CFS when they have learned how to decode, have fairly well-developed orthographic skills, and understand the reading.

The CFS was developed to chart reading rate as one of a battery of assessments administered to assess literacy. Even so, many teachers are uncomfortable assessing rate alone without fluency scale scores or comprehension questions. Fluency scale scores can easily be added to the CFS continuum. Blachowicz et al. (2001) suggest asking four comprehension questions after the reading and including that information with the continuum information (see Table 3.7).

The CFS information can be used to support fluency instruction in a few ways. First, it allows teachers to quickly view whose fluency rate is within, above, and below the average grade-level range. Some students may be reading too quickly, such as Courtney in Table 3.6, who read at 172 words correct per minute. Courtney's teacher assessed her further to ensure that her reading pace was not compromising comprehension. Other students may be reading at a rate so slow that they are not yet ready for explicit fluency instruction. Violet, Suzie, and Michael, in Table 3.6, are examples. With the information gleaned from this and other assessments, the teacher decided that Violet, Suzie, and Michael needed time and continued instruction in decoding and word automaticity before she would focus specifically on fluency. The last group of students—Becky, Ali, Vince, and Matt—were perfect candidates for explicit fluency instruction. These children had fluency rates below or close to the bottom of the grade-level range (60–90 words correct per minute for second grade), but also had fairly solid decoding and word recognition skills. In addition to participating in the whole-class fluency-building activities, these students would engage in individual and small-group lessons and activities that would promote fluent reading. Lastly, in addition to the information from other assessments, the CFS can be used to group students with similar needs for guided reading or flexible group instruction.

TABLE 3.7. Third-Grade Classroom Fluency Snapshot, Including Comprehension and Scale Scores

wcpm range	Student, wcpm rate	Comprehension	Expression/ volume	Phrasing	Smoothness	Pace
180	Will	4/4	4	4	4	4
175						
170						
165						
160	Valerie, 157	4/4	4	4	4	4
155						
150	Shaun, 149	4/4	3	4	4	4
	Sally, 147	4/4	3	4	4	4
145	Murray, 146	3/4	3	4	4	Too fast: A, E[a]
	Kelly, 144	4/4	3	4	3−	3
140	Ellie, 141	4/4	3	3+	3	3
135	Nick, 137	3/4	3−	3	2	3
	Tom, 137	4/4	3	4	4	4
	Zach, 132	3/4	3−	4−	4	4
130	Alfred, 129	3/4	3	4	4	4
125	Katie, 126	4/4	3−	4	4	3
120						
115	Paul, 115	4/4	3−	3	3	2
110						
105	Harry, 103	4/4	3	4	4	3
100	Alex, 100	3/4	2	2	2	2
95						
90	Alison, 92	2/4	3	3−	3−	3
85	Theo, 83	4/4	2	2	2	2
80	Alfie, 80	2/4	2+	2	3−	3
75	Shelly, 73	4/4	3	3	3−	3
70	Dayna, 70	2/4	1+	2	2	2
65						
60						

Note. CFS administered in May. The average third-grade words-correct-per-minute range is 80–120. Comprehension scores reflect the number answered correctly out of four questions. Scale scores reflect the Multidimensional Fluency Scale (Rasinski, 2004).
[a] The A and E scores for Murray reflect the Excessive Speed Reading (ESR) scale (Moskal, 2002).

Repeated Reading

A CFS is a perfect way to track fluency improvement three times during the school year, usually in September, January, and June. Repeated reading, on the other hand, allows teachers to continually track progress throughout the school year. In repeated reading, the same passage of 50–300 words is read two to three times in one session. Words-correct-per-minute rates and fluency scale scores are calculated for each of the three readings. In subsequent sessions the same passage is again read three times until a predetermined goal is met, and then the passage changes. A teacher is able to record progress in the readings of one passage, but also over passages of the same or increasingly higher levels.

Passages at an individual's instructional level are suggested when using repeated reading as an assessment tool. This means, in contrast to the CFS, the passages used for assessment vary because children have different reading levels. In addition, it is a good idea to use passages that include subject matter known to the reader. The steps of the repeated reading procedure can be found in Table 3.8; a detailed outline of the procedure follows. (See also Chapter 2 for a more in-depth discussion of repeated reading.)

Before beginning the assessment, count the number of words in the passage cumulatively by line to allow for a quick word count. Collect a stopwatch or watch with a second hand, two different colored pens or pencils, a blank sheet of paper or copy of the text to record miscues, and a calculator. Meet with the children one at a time and explain to each that this assessment allows you to help him or her become a better reader because the same passage is read by the child three times in a row. Read the title together and ask the child to talk a bit about what the author might include in the passage. Discuss the child's thoughts, and if the child doesn't seem to have enough background knowledge, change the passage selection.

Tell the student that you will be recording miscues so that you can support him or her for the rereading. In addition, explain that the reading is timed, and that the timer starts as soon as the child reads the first word of the passage. Say something like the following:

> "Read as well as you can to the end of the passage. After you read we will talk about how well you've read, and I will help you with any words that gave you trouble before you read again. I am going to time your reading, but I expect you to read at a normal pace, not too fast and not too slow. I will begin the timer when you say the first word. When you are ready, you can begin reading."

TABLE 3.8. Overview of Timed Repeated Reading Steps

Procedure

Select a passage of approximately 100–150 words. Mark the number of words cumulatively along the margin for easy counting.

The student reads orally while the being timed. Note where miscues occur. You can make a slash after 1 minute has passed, making sure that there are fewer than 15 errors (or 85%) within that minute. If there are more than 15 errors, the passage is too difficult.

Calculate the words-correct-per-minute rate:

Number of running words – number of miscues × 60 divided by 100 = wcpm rate

Review the miscues with the student.

The student rereads the same passage. Note the miscues and calculate the rate. Praise the child for improving and again review the miscues.

The student rereads the same passage once again. Note the miscues and calculate the rate. Praise the child for improvement.

Reread the same passage during the next session to a maximum of five repeated reading sessions with the same passage or until the child reaches or exceeds 100 words per minute with 98% accuracy.

Note. This procedure is appropriate for students at and above second grade.

While the child is reading, mark miscues on the copied passage or take a running record. As soon as the child finishes reading, record the time in seconds, the numbers of miscues, and the fluency scale scores. Ask the child, "How do you think you did? Do you remember any words that were difficult?" Give the child support with miscues and calculate a words-correct-per-minute rate. The formula for that calculation is:

$$\frac{(\text{Total number of words} - \text{total number of miscues}) \times 60}{\text{Total number of seconds}}$$

For example, say a 122-word passage was read in 111 seconds with 2 miscues. The calculation would be 122 words – 2 miscues = 120 words × 60 = 7,200 divided by 111 seconds equals 64.8 or 65 words correct per minute.

After talking about the miscues, the child rereads the same passage and the same procedures are followed for the second and third readings. Most of the time there is a decrease in the amount of miscues and an increase in rate from the first to second reading, and although there continues to be a decrease in miscues from the second to third readings, the increase in rate may be less dramatic. A record sheet, such as the example in Form 3.1, can be used to document fluency changes.

Teachers want to be able to document a consistent increase in reading rate on the first reading of texts on the same level used for the repeated reading activity. (For more information on leveled texts, see Fountas & Pinnell, 1999.) In other words, each time the child reads a new level N passage, the rate should increase slightly for the first reading of the passage. It is normal for the fluency rate to decrease as a student changes to a more difficult reading level. An increase of text level means the student may be reading passages with more content vocabulary, harder words to decode, longer sentences, or unfamiliar text structures. It is important to keep in mind that an accuracy rate should not fall below 85%. As a guide, remember that 15 miscues out of 100 words are 85%. When working with struggling readers, it is best to keep the accuracy closer to 90%, or 10 miscues out of 100 words. As levels increase in difficulty, remember to choose readings that match a child's background knowledge and allow for self-monitoring of comprehension.

Repeated reading can be used as an assessment of fluency and as a treatment for fluency development. As teachers assess and track fluency development through repeated readings, students benefit because repeated readings of the same passage develop oral reading fluency. It is a perfect, reciprocal activity!

Assessment of New and Previously Read Passages

There has been some debate as to whether children's fluency should be assessed using a new or previously read passage. Blachowicz et al. (2001) notes that the CFS profile doesn't seem to change much when using unread versus previously read materials as long as those materials previously read are not highly familiar.

With that finding in mind, some teachers have chosen to combine a fluency assessment with a benchmark comprehension assessment. Students are asked to read a school- or district-selected benchmark passage, and the reading is timed to calculate a words-correct-per-minute rate. A miscue analysis or running record is performed followed by an unassisted and assisted retelling, and comprehension questions. Finally, scoring from a fluency scale completes the fluency part of the assessment. In this way the teacher assesses word knowledge, comprehension, and fluency all at the same time.

FORM 3.1. REPEATED READING ASSESSMENT RECORD SHEET

Name _____

Title	Level	Date		No. of seconds	No. of miscues	wcpm rate	Expression	Phrasing	Smoothness	Pace
			1							
			2							
			3							
			1							
			2							
			3							
			1							
			2							
			3							

From *Partnering for Fluency* by Mary Kay Moskal and Camille Blachowicz. Copyright 2006 by The Guilford Press. Permission to photocopy this form is granted to purchasers of this book for personal use only (see copyright page for details).

Other teachers ask students to read the benchmark passage to assess decoding skills, word recognition, and comprehension, then a week or so later administer the CFS with the same passage to glean fluency information. The fluency information is then charted along a continuum to compare student ability. This method gives the children a chance to complete the fluency assessment with a previously read passage.

More important than assessing children on a new or familiar reading of a passage is that the *method of assessment* used stays consistent throughout the school year to allow for comparisons. Our recommendation is to use a cold reading of the same passage for the CFS three times during the school year (because of the time lag between the readings, the passage does not become familiar) and continue to gather information on fluency development by using new and familiar texts with repeated readings weekly or monthly.

TOM: A CASE STUDY

To see fluency assessment in action, let's look at the case of Tom. Tom is a fifth grader who enjoys mysteries. He reads at home and doesn't mind reading at school, especially when he can read a mystery novel. Tom's first language is Spanish, although he is fairly proficient in English. There are still some words he doesn't understand, but he'd rather not use a dictionary, he explained, because he can't always figure out what the definition means.

Background Information

Tom was given a battery of assessments in February of his fifth-grade year. He was able to represent most English phonemes correctly and was assessed to be in the syllables and affixes stage of spelling (Bear, Invernizzi, Templeton, & Johnston, 2004). Writing was an area of weakness, as was comprehension. On the Basic Reading Inventory (BRI; Johns, 2005) his instructional level was fifth grade for the narrative passage—which was a mystery! The expository selections began at the third-grade level, and the third-grade passage was very difficult for Tom. He was assessed to be at a frustration level.

Fluency Assessments

Tom's teacher used the BRI passages to assess his fluency. At the fifth-grade level he read the narrative passage at 104 words correct per minute and the third-grade expository passage at 96 words correct per minute. His reading was not described

Name Tom									
Title	Level	Date	No. of seconds	No. of miscues	wcpm rate	Expression	Phrasing	Smoothness	Pace
BRI Narrative Instructional	5th	2/10	53	8 Total 4 MC	104	2	3	2	3
BRI Expository Frustration	3rd	2/11	138	12 Total 6 MC	96	2	3	2	2

FIGURE 3.1. February fluency information for Tom. MC is a meaning change. The miscue changed the meaning of the text. The number of meaning changes are also included in the total number of miscues.

as fluent. Using the Multidimensional Fluency Scale, his ratings for the narrative passage included a 2 for expression, 3 for phrasing, 2 for smoothness, and 3 for pace. The expository passage included ratings of 2 for expression, 3 for phrasing, 2 for smoothness, and 2 for pace (see Figure 3.1). Finally, on the CFS using the school's benchmark passage, Tom ranked in the bottom quarter of the class on the continuum.

Fluency Assessment Analysis and Instructional Goals

Tom needed support in fluency. His rate was low for a fifth grader, especially when reading expository selections. His reading was choppy, relatively quiet, and he rarely used expression even when reading at an independent level. Tom's teacher set some fluency goals based on these assessments, which reflected the fluency he heard during class. First, Mr. Maloney wanted Tom's rate to increase. Although Tom's rate should be close to 150 words correct per minute by the end of the year, Mr. Maloney set a goal of 120 words correct per minute for narrative selections—a gain of approximately 5 words correct per minute for each of the remaining 3 months of the school year. Next, Mr. Maloney intended to help Tom make his reading smoother. Once he began to document an improvement, he integrated work on expression into the lessons. Finally, Mr. Maloney planned to work with expository texts, focusing instruction on both comprehension and fluency. His goal was to move Tom's instructional level and rate up at least one grade by June by means of working on both comprehension and fluency concurrently.

LOOKING AHEAD

Fluency assessment is the first step in planning for fluency instruction. With the understanding of how to assess fluency, it's time to practice. Choose about five or six students for whom you would like fluency information. Practice first with these students, and then slowly add others over time. Equipped with assessment information, let's now explore ways to prepare for fluency instruction in Chapter 4.

PREPARING FOR FLUENCY INSTRUCTION

W ith assessment information gathered both formally and informally, teachers are able to organize reading instruction to include various fluency development activities. This chapter considers planning and preparation for fluency development and instruction.

A STUDENT'S PERSPECTIVE OF FLUENCY INSTRUCTION

Children are better able to improve their fluency when they understand the goals of fluency instruction. They should be able to explain why the rereading of a passage is important to improve fluency, and after listening to a read-aloud, children should be able to discuss why a reading was fluent and how fluency was achieved. Teaching the characteristics of fluency—appropriate rate, accuracy, and prosody— is therefore the first step in fluency instruction and development.

To illustrate the importance of helping students understand the characteristics of fluency, consider two third-grade students who were working in pairs on repeated readings. One of the students began by reading a passage from her book but wanted to choose a different passage for the rereading. Asking her to explain why she wanted to read a different passage, she answered, "Well, because my goal

Students discuss a dysfluent oral reading to highlight the characteristics of fluency.

for the rereading is expression, and I want to make my voice go up and down—but wait, if I haven't read the words already, uh, it might be harder for me to do that. Oh, I get it! We reread [the same passage] so we can really concentrate on improving our fluency more than on reading the words!" This child knew the characteristics of fluency and therefore understood why it was best to stay with the same passage if she wanted to improve her expression.

STUDENTS NEED MODELS

Every young boy or girl who wants to become a star athlete has a favorite role model. He wants to "be like Mike [Jordan]," she wants to serve like Serena Williams or to pass like Mia Hamm, he wants to pitch like Mark Prior. In the same way, students need models of fluency to help them understand their goal. To begin thinking about fluency, children should be exposed to both fluent and dysfluent models of reading. One way for children to learn about the characteristics of fluency is to ask them to listen to a recording that includes the reading of the same passage several times in several different ways. This one passage is read too fast, too slowly, fluently, word by word, with incorrect phrasing, with incorrect intonation, ignoring punctuation, with miscues and repetition, and fluently again. Students are asked to evaluate the reading and their comments are recorded on chart paper for future reference. The discussion of the fluent and dysfluent renditions allow for a common fluency vocabulary and models to which teachers can refer when discussing oral reading.

Just as it is important to present curriculum standards to students in a friendly language to help them understand learning goals, fluency terminology should also be composed of student-friendly language. Using the children's language, terms and phrases describing fluent reading are then used along with words such as *phrasing, expression*, and *pace* to support the children's awareness of what they should strive to accomplish with fluency activities. For example, after hearing the tape of fluent and dysfluent reading, one second grader described fluent reading as sounding like talking: "That wasn't too fast, and there was expression, and it sounded like she was talking to me!" Afterward, the children used "sounded like talking" to assess their use of expression.

Although teachers can model a passage read aloud both fluently and dys-fluently for this initial activity, it is preferable to use a tape-recorded passage of various fluent/dysfluent readings because the reading stays consistent and can be revisited during different times throughout the school year for continued discussion. Helping students verbalize their own goals comes next. On one occasion Kendal, a second grader, chose reading faster as his fluency goal. Given this misdirected goal, his fluency began to suffer because the reading was much too fast. In a small group of four children, including Kendal, students listened to the prerecorded fluency tape once again and were instructed to comment on each of the readings. When they heard the passage read much too quickly, all four children began to giggle and talk at once, "There's no expression! It's too fast!" Kendal even commented that the fluency of the reader was below any rating he could have given. After this discussion, Kendal changed. His readings became more articulate and fluent. When asked to comment on the transformation, Kendal said, "Well, I've been reading slower than before because my reading was *way* too fast. I wasn't thinking right" (Moskal, 2002, p. 116). In this example Kendal figured out what he needed to do when reading aloud, realizing that he had been reading too fast.

Once students have a concept of fluency and vocabulary to describe their goals, provide models by letting them listen to taped readings and by reading to them to make sure that they *hear* good reading. Too often readers who are not fluent spend significant time in groups with other students who are also not fluent, so that they never hear how good reading actually sounds. Most commercial reading programs have tapes available that match the reading selections in basal anthologies and in small books that accompany a reading series. These are invaluable as a first step in working with a passage for fluency practice. Also a number of publishers offer audiotaped versions of some trade books that are used in literacy instruction, and national organizations provide taped books and materials for students with disabilities (e.g., Recording for the Blind and Dyslexic at www.rfbd.org/).

SELECTING APPROPRIATE PASSAGES FOR FLUENCY DEVELOPMENT

When choosing passages for fluency development, there are five considerations: (1) the incidence of content words and high-frequency words, (2) the language patterns, (3) familiarity with the topic, (4) the number of words in the passage, and (5) the level of the text. Each is important, especially with average and struggling readers, to ensure not only a productive learning experience but also a positive one.

The two passages in Tables 4.1 and 4.2 have the same readability to illustrate some of the considerations when choosing texts for fluency development. Not all passages will work equally well. *A Giant Panda's Story* is an example of a good choice, whereas the Junie B. Jones books, which are very engaging and adored by young children, are not suitable for fluency work. These two passage samples, *A Giant Panda's Story* and *Junie B. Jones Is a Graduation Girl* (Park, 2001), are highlighted in some of the following sections.

TABLE 4.1. An Appropriate Passage for Fluency Practice

A Giant Panda's Story

The giant panda lives in a mountain forest in China. She roams the forest, happy to be alone. But in early fall she finds a den in the rocky sides of the mountain. She makes a nest in her den to give birth to her cub.

When the giant panda cub is born he needs his mother. The cub is very tiny at birth. He weighs just five ounces and has fine, or thin, white fur. The mother panda holds her cub close to her body to keep it warm.

When the cub is one month old he looks more like his mother. His fur becomes thick, and black and white. He still cannot crawl or walk. But the mother panda can now leave the cub for a short time to get food. She rushes back when she hears the cub's loud cry. It sounds just like a baby.

Note. Reprinted by permission of the author, Diane Sullivan.

Content and High-Frequency Words

It makes sense that the more frequently a reader is exposed to a word, the easier the word is to learn and recall. Furthermore, words following regular decoding rules that are easy to sound out assist a reader in fast and easy word recognition. Both high-

TABLE 4.2. A Passage That Is Less Desirable for Fluency Practice

Junie B. Jones Is a Graduation Girl

Just then, I sat up very fast. 'Cause I was getting another brainstorm in my head, I believe. I zoomed straight to my desk. Then I looked through all my drawers. And I found my colored markers. I laughed real happy. Then I spread my graduation gown on the floor. And I worked and worked very hard. And guess what? When I finally got done, you couldn't even spot the driblets, hardly!

Note. From Park (2001, pp. 49–50). Copyright 2001 by Barbara Park. Reprinted by permission of Random House Children's Books, a division of Random House, Inc.

frequency words (words encountered frequently in text) and decodable words (words that are easy to decode) facilitate comprehension and fluency because the cognitive demands of the reader are not strained in reading.

When choosing text for fluency instruction, the number of high-frequency and decodable words should be a factor. Hiebert and Fisher (2002) considered texts used to teach first graders how to read and measured the kinds of words in the stories. Using a measurement called critical word factor, the researchers investigated the demands of a reader in word recognition and decoding. They found that when words are new or "unique"— that is, when they fall outside the range of high frequency and easily decoded—comprehension and fluency are compromised. Using texts with too many new words interferes with understanding and fluency.

To choose suitable texts, teachers should look for books that (1) have words that are encountered many times, and (2) follow phonetically regular rules. In doing so, students can improve their word recognition skills, ultimately leading to enhanced fluency and comprehension. The ability to read words with accuracy is related to reading levels, described next.

Take a look at the two passage samples. *Junie B. Jones Is a Graduation Girl* (Park, 2001) does include some common words, but there are many words that are less common, such as *brainstorm, zoomed, believed, graduation,* and *driblets.* In contrast, *A Giant Panda's Story* contains common words that all follow regular phonetic rules, making it the better choice.

Language Patterns and Topic Familiarity

When making passage selections for fluency development, it is important to consider both (1) language patterns and (2) student's prior knowledge of a reading selection topic. It is best to choose readings for fluency development that feature natural language patterns. Natural language patterns support correct phrasing and fluency in general, given that children are already familiar with oral language patterns. For example, two simple sentences can demonstrate a slight but powerful difference:

> Mother, I do not see my school bag on the table.
>
> Mother, I don't see my backpack on the table.

Both are about equal difficulty, but the second uses a contraction more likely to be used in real language and the term "backpack," which is more common in American English.

Students can make predictions from language patterns and vocabulary that are natural. Briggs and Forbes (2002) give the example "*I have a* _____," (p. 3). English-speaking children predict that a singular noun follows the sentence starter, possibly preceded by an adjective. Predicting language patterns is another skill that supports fluency and comprehension.

Take a look at the passage samples again. The language patterns in *Junie B. Jones* (Park, 2001) are more difficult to read. The structure of the sentences *'Cause I was getting another brainstorm in my head, I believe* (p. 49) and *When I finally got done, you couldn't even spot the driblets, hardly!* (p. 50) are not predictable. In contrast, the sentences in *A Giant Panda's Story* are very natural and highly predictable (e.g., *The cub is very tiny at birth*).

Just as prior knowledge, or familiarity with the reading topic, supports comprehension, it also supports fluency. The ability to predict, anticipate, and make text connections (Allington, 2001; Briggs & Forbes, 2002) helps support fluent reading. Think of how fluency is affected when reading an unfamiliar topic. The reading is slower and can be dysfluent because the reader needs to decode and decipher new vocabulary as well as try to maintain understanding and possibly deal with an unfamiliar text pattern. Prior knowledge and familiarity contribute to the ability to read fluently.

Both passage examples include topics familiar to students. Kindergarten graduations, the topic of *Junie B. Jones Is a Graduation Girl* (Park, 2001), are common and many young children have participated in one. Pandas are also familiar to children because of their popularity. Pandas are seen on television, in zoos, and some children may even own a toy panda.

Number of Words in a Passage

Generally, passages used for fluency instruction and development range from 50 to 300 words (Dowhower, 1989). In deciding a suitable passage length for students of various grade levels at different ability levels, one option is to consider the length of time the children are allotted for fluency development and adjust appropriately. For example, one group of second graders were assessed to have fluency rates that ranged from 22 to 34 words correct per minute. Their teacher wanted them to reread passages after a guided reading session in which she used materials that posed enough of a challenge without being too difficult. With their words-correct-per-minute range in mind, along with 10 minutes allotted for rereading activity, the teacher decided that a 50- to 60-word passage would be appropriate. In that same classroom, students whose rates ranged from 90 to 110 were assigned passages of about 100 to 115 words for the same 10 minutes.

This second-grade teacher decided to plan for a "chamber theater" (Wolf, 1994) activity. In chamber theater children combine choral reading, readers' theatre, and mime into a presentation. The teacher decided on passages of 300 words for groups of four children; the practice sessions would span a week. Children of all reading levels would have enough time to rehearse reading the lines to present a dramatic, fluent reading of the text.

Matching Students to the Level of Text

Stanovich (2000) asserts that the quick and automatic recognition of words allows a reader to focus cognitive attention on processes such as understanding and fluency. With this point in mind, it is clear that fluency development is enhanced when readers are matched with materials that allow them to read with ease (Strecker et al., 1998).

Because students are able to concentrate on fluent reading when word recognition is not an issue, an accuracy level is used to determine the difficulty of a passage for fluency instruction (Rasinski, 1989). There are different views of accuracy levels and text difficulty in relation to fluency development. Dowhower (1987) recommends an 85% accuracy rate for fluency development, whereas Guszak (1992) believes a 95% accuracy rate is better. In order to make an informed decision regarding the appropriate accuracy level for fluency instruction, consider reading levels instead.

Betts (1954) suggests using reading levels described as *independent*, *instructional*, and *frustration* to guide the selection of passages for various reading instruction purposes, including fluency development. These levels are based on reading accuracy. Frustration-level passages are too difficult for a student to read; such passages result in an accuracy level below 90% or one error for every 10 words. Although it is commonly thought that children should not ever read at a frustration level for instructional purposes, Kuhn and Stahl (2000) report that with repeated readings and direct, guided assistance and feedback from a knowledgeable teacher, students are able to improve their fluency with frustration-level materials.

An independent level allows for reading ease with five errors or less per 100 words. Clay (2002) suggests that the accuracy level for independent reading is 95–100%; this range is a commonly used guideline. Children working independently or with peers to improve fluency, instead of working with teachers and adults, should work at the independent level (Moskal, 2002), at which they have little trouble with word recognition and are therefore able to focus on phrasing and prosody (Barr, Blachowicz, Katz, & Kaufman, 2002).

Instructional-level passages have a 90–94% accuracy rate (Clay, 2002). It is at this level, which poses an appropriate challenge without being too difficult, that much explicit fluency instruction occurs. The key is the scaffolding provided by the teacher to support any difficulty with word recognition (Kuhn & Stahl, 2000) and then to support other fluency goals.

Consider the example of a Sue, a second grader (Blachowicz, et al., 2000). Sue read three different passages (text 1, text 2, text 3) three times in a repeated reading activity. Table 4.3 contains an analysis of Sue's accuracy, rate, and self-assessed use of punctuation and expression. It should be fairly easy to ascertain which readings are at her frustration, instructional, and independent levels—but at which level should fluency instruction be focused? Look to see the level at which there was consistent improvement in accuracy, rate, punctuation usage, and expression over the three readings. Did you guess text 2? Because there is consistent improvement at the instructional level, it is the level where fluency instruction tends to take place.

Here are a few guidelines when considering text levels for fluency development:

➢ Accuracy levels should remain at 90% or above. With the ability to read words with ease, more energy can be directed toward reading fluently.

➢ Reading at the independent level allows children to focus on fluency instead of decoding and strategy practice. It also affords children the opportunity to work in pairs to support each other in developing fluency.

➢ Instructional-level texts should be paired with comprehension and fluency activities guided by the teacher. In this way children practice integrating the processes needed for comprehension and fluent reading.

➢ Although it is recommended that students never be asked to read at their frustration levels (Briggs & Forbes, 2002), Kuhn and Stahl (2000) suggest that fluency can improve at that level, given explicit and intense support.

TABLE 4.3. Sue's Profile: Three Readings of Leveled Texts

	Miscues	wcpm rate	Student self-assessed use of punctuation[a]	Student self-assessed use of expression[a]
Text 1 (126 words)				
First reading	16	41	3	3
Second reading	13	56	4	3
Third reading	15	46	3	3
Text 2 (124 words)				
First reading	9	46	3	3
Second reading	8	58	4	5
Third reading	1	75	5	5
Text 3 (15 words)				
First reading	2	82	5	5
Second reading	1	93	5	5
Third reading	0	100	5	5

Note. The average words-correct-per-minute range for second grade is 60–90. From Blachowicz, Fisher, Obrochta, Massarelli, Moskal, and Jones (2000).
[a] Scale of 5–1, with 5 meaning "always," and 1 meaning "never."

For further assistance in matching students to the level of text, a good resource teachers can use is *Matching Books to Readers* (Fountas & Pinnell, 1999). Other resources for teachers include:

Gunning, T. G. (1998). *Best books for beginning readers*. Needham Heights, MA: Allyn & Bacon.—This book provides a compilation of more than 1,000 high-quality children's books from the emergent to the grade-2 reading levels.

Fountas, I. C., & Pinnell, G. S. (1996). *Guided reading*. Portsmouth, NH: Heinemann.—This book includes a long list of many popular books from a variety of publishers with the corresponding reading level.

Peterson, B. (1991). Selecting books for beginning readers. In D. E. DeFord, C. A. Lyons, & G. S. Pinnell (Eds.), *Bridges to literacy: Learning from Reading Recovery*. Portsmouth, NH: Heinemann.—This chapter describes the 20 different reading levels used to level Reading Recovery books. A bibliography of books at each level is included.

There are also numerous websites which contain bibliographies of fluency materials for children:

American Library Association Recommended Books for Children—www.ala.org/ala/alsc/
    alscresources/summerreading/recsummerreading/recommendedreading.htm
Reading Rockets Monthly Recommendations—www.readingrockets.org/books/
    booksbytheme.php
Booklist of the Cooperative Children's Book Center—www.soemadison.wisc.edu/ccbc/
    books/default.asp

TO FURTHER FLUENCY DEVELOPMENT

One of the first steps in preparing for fluency instruction is to include the children
in the goals for fluency development. Students should learn and use the terminology of fluency, which will help them understand the characteristics to incorporate
into a fluent reading. Passage selection is important in fluency instruction. The
number of words, type of words, text levels, language patterns, and familiarity with
the subject matter are all factors to consider when planning fluency lessons. Now
that you are ready, Chapter 5 offers lessons that promote fluency development.

FLUENCY LESSONS

When planning for fluency instruction, teachers should consider activities for individuals, pairs, small groups, and the whole class. Of course, a classroom of 20 students means that there are, most likely, 20 unique fluency profiles ranging from fluent to dysfluent. How can a teacher begin to support the fluency needs of individual students in a class? Individual fluency needs can be supported by varying the types of fluency lessons. This chapter introduces some of the instructional activities that support fluency development in classrooms that are typically comprised of diverse learners. Chapter 6 examines fluency development with student partners.

DAILY FLUENCY MODELING ACTIVITIES

Teacher-Led Read-Alouds

There was a range of literacy and fluency development in Julie's third-grade classroom (see the CFS in Table 3.7). Julie wanted an activity that would support all reading levels, develop comprehension and fluency (among other things), and challenge each student in a whole-class activity. What did Julie do? The answer is quite simple; Julie read aloud every day (Stahl, 1996)! Reading aloud models a fluent rendition of the text. Teachers who read with phrasing and pauses, allowing their voices to be loud, soft, high, and low, are drawing attention to the use of prosody to model a dramatic interpretation of the reading. In addition, readers share their interpretations of the text by using the voice to show the meaning of a reading (Rasinski, 2004). Frequently children describe this interpretation as reading that "sounds like talking."

In a recent study (Moskal, 2005), the fluency development of two third-grade classrooms was compared. In one class the teacher read aloud at least once a day but frequently more often. By springtime, most students had internalized the model of dramatic reading used by the teacher and the students' oral readings were found to be more expressive than those in the comparison group. The students appeared to be influenced by their teacher's prosodic oral reading and read to mimic it themselves.

Teachers can also read aloud to begin a small-group guided reading lesson. This read-aloud can be followed by skill or strategy instruction, student reading for deeper understanding, a follow-up discussion, and a fluency development activity. In this way, the teacher provides a model of how fluent reading should sound and ensures that comprehension is the focus of reading. In contrast, some teachers end

Reading aloud before instructional groupings facilitates fluency and comprehension.

a guided reading session with a read-aloud of the same text just read for instructional purposes. Reading after the children are familiar with the story allows their attention to focus on the model of fluent oral reading instead of primarily making meaning.

There is one important step, often ignored, that allows for a successful teacher read-aloud. To guarantee an expressive, fluent reading, the text should be practiced before reading it to the students.

Student-Led Read-Alouds

Cathy is another third-grade teacher who wants her students to read fluently. Many of her students, including a few English learners, struggle with reading. Like others in her school, Cathy provides time for the students to select books to read during a silent sustained reading (SSR) time. Cathy also provides a separate time when the students read aloud for fluency building. "They know their goal is to practice, practice, practice, and they really seem to enjoy it," explains Cathy.

The children use the passages they read during guided reading to practice. They find a spot in the room and read aloud to themselves, rereading paragraphs or pages at a time until they hear themselves reading smoothly with few errors. While they are reading, Cathy walks around the room, stopping to listen to each child for a minute or so. The children learning to read in English work directly with Cathy's assistant. They too read and reread, but there is more of an emphasis on continued support of understanding.

Twice a month, the children prepare to read aloud to others in the school community. Instead of reading to themselves, they read to the principal, secretaries, fine arts teachers, gym teachers, and librarians. They sometimes pair up with kindergartners or fifth graders to read too. It's an exciting time for them because their hard work pays off! They are to read fluently and shine in front of others!

VOCABULARY VISITS

Vocabulary is often a stumbling block to fluency. Blachowicz and Obrochta (2005) suggest a method of using read-alouds with content-area material to develop vocabulary knowledge. These same read-alouds can provide models for reading informational materials. Text sets focused around a topic, such as weather, the human body, communities, and so forth, provide repetition of vocabulary that makes learning and becoming fluent easier. This scaffolded read-aloud process has two steps: Jump Start and First Write. After selecting a topical text set of 5 books, the teacher gives the class a Jump Start to help them activate their prior knowledge. She introduces the topic and asks students to talk, briefly, about some things they know about it. Then students take a piece of paper and do a First Write, listing words that they can connect to the topic. These lists are archived in folders and serve as a preassessment. First Write is also a good diagnostic tool for teachers and can provide surprising insights. Speaking about one very shy and quiet first grader, a teacher remarked, "I didn't know Keisha knew so much about animals. It turns out she goes to the zoo almost every other week with her daddy. I'll really have to draw on that in the discussions."

Group Talk

The next step is Group Talk. Students gather on the rug as the teacher brings out a poster depicting a topic and starts with the first question, "What do you see?" just as the teacher would do on a regular field trip. As students contribute words related to what they see, the teacher records their contributions on Post-its and places them on the poster. For example, after reviewing a skeleton chart, the first word that came from the group was *skull*, and the teacher used a Post-it to place the word on a relevant place on the chart. The second word to come up was *cranium*, which amazed the teacher. The children then informed her that "Cranium" was a game that was advertised for the holidays and that was in the school game collection. This word led to *head* and then *crown*, followed by a chorus of *Jack* and *Jill*.

As students suggest new additions, the teacher's job is to mediate, as needed. For example, the teacher makes sure that the targeted vocabulary is generated by supporting the students' learning with questions, explanations, and suggestions. "Touch your skull. What is a skull for?" ("To protect your brain.") Add *brain* and *protect*. "How does it protect it?" led to the word *hollow* for skull. The teacher then asked for an example of *hollow*, which was supplied by a student who described being surprised to find that his chocolate Easter bunny wasn't solid chocolate. "Yeah, I hate that," agreed some of his classmates.

The words come thick and fast, and the teacher's job is to focus on the important ones, ask for clarification and example ("Where is your wrist?"), and group them in some relational way. Other senses besides sight are used. For example, in the visit about weather, the teacher asked, "What do you hear in a storm? What are some words for how you feel in rain?" After 5–10 minutes, there are usually quite a number of words on the chart that the students have now heard, seen, discussed, and sometimes acted out.

Reading and Thumbs Up

The next step is the reading of the first book. Reading aloud to students has been found to be a significant way to increase vocabulary (Blachowicz & Obrochta, 2005). However, research suggests that this reading should include mediation for new words and should not be a dramatic performance (Dickinson & Smith, 1994). Rather it should be like the kind of reading a parent does with a child, sometimes stopping to clarify or ask about something, much as the highly popular Richard Scarry books call for labeling and finding. We use the "thumbs up" procedure to help cultivate active listeners. Students put their thumbs up when they hear a new word. Sometimes the teacher stops or rereads a sentence when no thumbs go up for a critical term, but the goal is to have a fairly normal reading experience.

After the reading students discuss what they learned and add a few new words to the chart. If time permits, the teacher sometimes initiates semantic sorting activities with the words as well as bringing in more of the senses. For example, for a unit on weather, the teacher asked, after reading the first book, if there were "sound" words that the students associated with thunderstorms, and connected *crash, boom, thunder, thunderclap*, and other words, some from the book and some from personal knowledge.

Finally, a short writing activity occurs; students write about something learned or something that particularly interested them. The books are also put in a central location for reading during independent reading time, and students are asked to read at least one of the books each week and to record it in their reading logs. One teacher noted, "These books circulate four or five times more than they did last year. The read-alouds help my kids get interested in the topic and also makes the other books accessible to them because they know some of the ideas and the vocabulary. It really works!"

Follow-Up

The visit poster is kept on the wall and the read-aloud, thumbs up, adding words, and semantic sorting and writing activities are repeated for each book in the set. The students also add new words to the chart on their own and sometimes regroup the words. Over the course of the unit, students apply their new word knowledge through extension activities that include semantic sorting, word games, writing, reading new books on the same topic, and rereading the books the teacher has read. One participating teacher also observed, "My students began making up some of their own activities. They would take the Post-its and put them in new sets or make sentences with them. They got interested in the new words and proud that they knew such grown-up ones."

Final Write

At the end of the entire five-book sequence, the students engage in two varieties of writing activities. One is a book or report about their learning. In some classes, for example, students make their own books about the skeletal system to take home or put in their classroom libraries. In others, students do a report on their favorite book. In first grade, this report is often in the form of "The three most interesting things . . . " or "What the author could do to make this book better . . . " (D. Gurvitz, personal communication, November 7, 2000), rather than using a contrived book report form.

Students also do a Final Write, a list-writing activity of all the words they now can write associated with a topic. Their lists increase dramatically from First Write. Those students who list the fewest vocabulary words at the beginning of the visit usually make the greatest gains, but even those starting with richer initial vocabularies make significant gains. Teachers can also evaluate word learning by students' uses of the words in these final activities. Another anecdotal bit of evaluation may come from parents' reports of new word use and requests to get books on the teacher's topics from the library and bookstores.

The next section of this chapter highlights fluency activities that are easily incorporated into a literacy curriculum. The lessons are divided into whole class, small group, student pairs, and teacher–student pairs. Of course, this doesn't mean the lessons must be taught in the grouping suggested. The settings are flexible and the lessons are adaptable for different curricula and fluency needs.

SUGGESTIONS FOR WHOLE-CLASS FLUENCY LESSONS

Choral Reading

Have you ever seen children sitting together and reading in unison? That is choral reading. Choral reading allows students to participate relatively risk free as they read collectively with the group. Or they can just listen until they feel confident enough to join in the reading. The reading material selected for this activity is fun and engaging, and the children look forward to it.

Choral reading promotes fluency because a fluent reader—most often the teacher—models the first reading and guides subsequent readings of the text. Children then practice as a group to read accurately, smoothly, and with prosody. With repeated choral readings, the fluent reading becomes automatic. Dysfluent children are more willing to participate because they hear a fluent rendition and can participate without drawing attention to themselves. In addition, the reading materials chosen for choral reading should allow for an enjoyable and meaningful fluency activity that encourages all to participate.

It is best when texts for choral reading are presented in a format that is easy for large groups to read. Each child might have a copy of the text to be read together, or the teacher might refer to an enlarged version of the text printed on chart paper. In the primary grades, big books are often used for choral reading activities in what is called a shared book experience (Dorn, French, & Jones, 1998). If the children are all reading from one large text, the print needs to be sizeable so that the words can be read from a distance. Texts for choral reading can be provided on an overhead, but it is a good idea to also provide a copy that the children can have right in front of them.

Steps for Instruction

Children sit so that they can view the selection to be read together. A new text is read first by the teacher, who models the reading at a natural pace while the children follow along with their eyes. The teacher reads the text a second time and offers an invitation to the students to read along if and when they feel comfortable. If most children read along during the second reading, the teacher asks everyone to join in on the third reading. If few join the second reading, "invitational" reading continues until most students seem to be ready to chime in. By the third rereading, though, most students are confident enough to read with the group.

In many classes there is a designated choral reading time when children read old favorites together and are introduced to new passages. As the children get used to the choral reading format, a student can lead the reading of familiar texts while the teacher guides the new readings.

Teacher Tips

➤ *Daily class choral.* The teacher presents a passage, written on laminated chart paper, that expresses some emotion, such as fear or surprise, for a week of choral reading. The teacher first reads the passage, often selected from a chapter book used for reading aloud to the class, allowing for a fluent rendition. The students then read the passage chorally on Monday. Each day the class takes a 3- to 5-minute pause for choral reading. On Wednesday students receive a copy of the passage for their class choral folders and continue with the daily choral reading, actively participating with, for example, a fearful or surprised tone. Twice a month the regular silent sustained reading becomes *company choral*, as partners or small groups read selected passages from their class choral folders aloud, in unison, in place of individual silent reading.

> ### SIMPLE STEPS: CHORAL READING
> 1. Select an engaging text and present it to students in an enlarged format.
> 2. Model the reading while the children listen.
> 3. Read the text again and invite students to join in the reading.
> 4. Invite all students to join the choral reading by the third or fourth rereading.

➤ *School share.* Schools that focus on choral reading for fluency often have different classes do their choral reading over the PA each day. This approach provides an audience for the sharing and models good reading for the other students in the school as well. Students love to perform, and this is a very motivating activity.

➤ *Home tapes.* After a choral passage has been performed in school, the teacher can send students home with a tape as a home–school connection activity. In some classrooms the family then does a choral reading of the passage and returns the tape to school for further listening. These can be done on audiotapes or CDs; some ambitious families send videos of their performance. This activity builds a library of tapes for the classroom as well.

Fluency Development Lesson

Although children hear and practice fluent renditions of shared texts in choral reading, the fluency development lesson (Opitz, Rasinski, & Bird, 1998) is a more direct way of teaching fluency and its characteristics. This lesson combines whole-group instruction and choral reading practice with individual practice and feedback. It is an effective way of teaching the components of fluent reading (accuracy, pace, and prosody) and giving students the time to practice reading not only with an emphasis on those components, but also to practice using the vocabulary of fluency in an authentic situation.

In a fluency development lesson, the teacher leads the class in a discussion about an aspect of fluency development. A passage is projected onto the overhead, and the fluency focus is demonstrated.

For example, Bill Martin Jr.'s (1983) *Brown Bear, Brown Bear, What Do You See?* ("Brown Bear, Brown Bear, / What do you see? / I see a redbird / Looking at me.") is a book composed of a series of questions and responses. This text is a natural resource for discussing the role of punctuation in prosody. Each question should be read with a rising tone at the end. The responses are read with a falling sound. The teacher models the process and makes sure students understand the role of punctuation.

Then the passage is passed out to the students, who read it chorally, practicing the fluency aspect demonstrated. Next, children work as partners to practice reading aloud to each other, using the same passage. Student assessment has a distinctive role in this lesson, as partners critique the oral readings.

The benefits of the fluency development lesson are several. The teacher models fluency and invites the students to practice together in choral reading. Familiar with the passage, student pairs practice improving fluency with rereading. Children are invested in the activity because the self-assessment component is motivating and student centered.

Steps for Instruction

The goal of this sample fluency development lesson is to highlight appropriate phrasing. Using a passage on an overhead projector, the teacher first reads it aloud as the children follow along. The teacher guides the children's thinking by asking questions about the use of punctuation and how punctuation helps the listener understand the reading. Next the teacher elaborates with examples of how sentences are parsed into chunks to show meaning even when the sentence contains no commas—for example, *The lazy dog/jumps over/the large brown fence.* The teacher leads the class in slashing phrase boundary lines in a series of examples from the passage and invites the class to read the passage chorally, using the slash marks to guide their reading.

Next the children receive copies of the passage and are divided into pairs to take turns reading and rereading it. The listening partner offers the reading partner words of encouragement and support between the first and second reading. Before switching roles, the reader fills out an assessment form to reflect on the fluency of the reading (see Forms 5.1 and 5.2 for examples). The children are directed to use the correct fluency vocabulary when discussing the readings and filling out the self-assessment forms.

Teacher Tips

➢ When children become familiar with the activity, it takes only about 20 minutes and therefore can easily be a weekly addition to the literacy curriculum.

➢ Consider pairing students to read together for an entire month before changing partners. This duration not only helps the activity to run smoothly, but also builds student relationships and classroom community.

➢ Model the kind of talk that should occur between partners as they support each other. In addition, brainstorm words and phrases that can be used in fill-

FORM 5.1. FLUENCY ASSESSMENT FORM A

FLUENCY RATING

Circle your fluency goal for this reading:

Pace Accuracy Phrasing Expression

I met my goal:

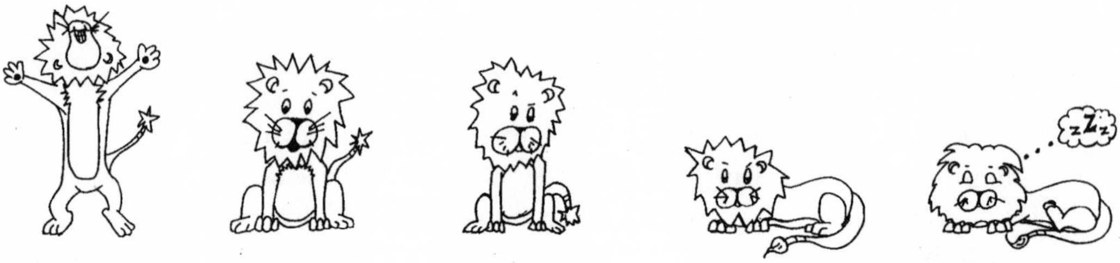

Drawings by C. Sassetti, 2004

My thoughts: ______________________________

____

____

____

____

____

____

FORM 5.2. FLUENCY ASSESSMENT FORM B

FLUENCY CHECK

Rate your fluency:

Drawings by C. Sassetti, 2004

This is something I did well: _____

_____

_____

_____

This is something I can work on to improve: _____

_____

_____

_____

SIMPLE STEPS:
FLUENCY DEVELOPMENT LESSON

1. The teacher highlights a fluency characteristic with the whole class.

2. A passage is used to demonstrate the application of the fluency characteristic.

3. The students read the passage chorally to practice the fluency characteristic.

4. The same passage is used as student pairs practice reading and rereading to develop the fluency focus.

5. Student pairs assess their fluency progress.

ing out the student assessment sheets. This activity also acts as a review of the fluency characteristics.

Readers' Theatre

Readers' Theatre is a performance of reading in which the focus is to use one's voice to present a dramatic interpretation of a script or text. The performance is perfect for a classroom setting because little is necessary other than the script itself. Children neither memorize lines nor use costumes, props, or designed sets (Martinez, Roser, & Strecker, 1998/1999). Performers stand in front of the audience (i.e., the class) holding their scripts and read the story aloud, interpreting their parts using stress (volume) and intonation (pitch). Even though students work on scripts in small groups, Readers' Theatre is included in whole-class fluency instruction because most teachers schedule an exclusive time when the whole class works at the same time.

Children involved in Readers' Theatre activities improve oral fluency and deepen their understanding because rereading is mandatory for rehearsals. Martinez, Roser, and Strecker (1998/1999) found that second graders made significant reading gains after a 10-week period of Readers' Theatre rehearsals and productions. Students enjoy Readers' Theatre not only because it is fun and purposeful, but also because they can hear how their reading becomes expressive with continued practice.

Steps for Instruction

When working with a whole class, a range of leveled books can be used so that the text is not too difficult for any group of children. Reading materials are then transformed into a script format. Narrative scripts include characters and one or more narrators, whereas expository scripts are divided into voices or speakers. Initially

Third graders perform using a Readers' Theatre script.

the scripting should be done by the teacher, but as children become familiar with the activity, they can be taught the scripting process and given a book or passage that they script in groups. The benefits double when children script texts because they deepen their understanding and ability to read fluently as they collaboratively create the theatre they eventually perform in front of a real audience.

Readers' Theatre scripts are also available on the Web and in published texts. These are useful when the time necessary for scripting is limited. Many of the published scripts are good to excellent in quality, although it may be difficult to accurately level the scripts for readers of various abilities. Nonetheless, for a teacher interested in trying Readers' Theatre, published scripts may be a better place to start.

To prepare for the performance, set aside a period of time each day as all the children practice the scripts in small groups. It is suggested that children first read through the script chorally. Next, children read the entire script practicing different lines without yet being assigned a character. In this step children discuss how a line might be read; should the reader emphasize one word, should the voice go up, should a section be read quietly or in a whiney voice? After negotiating how the text might be read, characters or voices can be chosen or assigned and rehearsal for the performance can begin.

The time necessary to rehearse varies. Some teachers use a weekly schedule whereby groups read the entire script on Mondays and perform it on Fridays. Other teachers develop a performance schedule and groups sign up when they are ready to perform in front of an audience. Either way, the power of Readers' Theatre as a tool for fluency development is clear. Children become deeply involved in understanding the text and conveying that understanding to the audience through a fluent reading. Readers' Theatre is a most effective activity.

Teacher Tips

➢ Take the show on the road! Put a sign up in the teachers' lounge so that the Readers' Theatre ensemble can go on tour.

➢ Using leveled Readers' Theatre texts means that ensemble groups usually stay the same. To mix groups, occasionally use easy-to-read texts so that groups can be heterogeneous. Another idea is to script for a whole-class Readers' Theatre instead of small-group performances. This way the leveling is achieved simply by the amount and difficulty of the scripted parts. In other words, assign less able readers easy lines and more capable readers the most difficult parts.

➢ Most production difficulties arise from children reading quietly and/or holding the script in front of the face. Children should be aware of these issues while rehearsing.

SIMPLE STEPS: READERS' THEATRE

1. A script is selected or a text is transformed into a script.
2. Students read the entire script chorally.
3. Individuals practice reading lines, and the group discusses the various ways the lines can be interpreted through expressive reading.
4. Characters or voices are assigned or chosen.
5. Rehearsals begin and the performance is given once the group is ready.

In addition to reading aloud in Readers' Theatre, the fluency development lesson, and choral reading, teachers can use flexible grouping techniques to streamline fluency instruction. By referring to a CFS that includes words correct per minute and Multidimensional Fluency Scale scores, a teacher can group children to focus on particular needs. For example, a group of children may need assistance with phrasing. The teacher can work with these students as a small group to introduce activities that promote proper phrasing. The following section highlights fluency lessons appropriate for small groups.

SUGGESTIONS FOR SMALL-GROUP FLUENCY LESSONS

Radio Reading

Radio reading is an activity that allows students to prepare a portion of connected text to be read aloud in a small group setting, acting as either a broadcaster (reader) or audience (listener). The activity can take the place of round robin reading in instructional or guided reading. First students practice reading to themselves, then they read aloud to the group. Individual readers have a chance to hear themselves read smoothly and effortlessly while modeling fluent reading for their "audience."

Steps for Instruction

A text is selected and students are encouraged to share what they know about the topic. The teacher can either give an overview of the selection or ask students to predict what the reading may include. Students are assigned a portion of the text to prepare when they take on the role of the broadcaster and are then asked to read the entire passage to themselves. After reading the passage, individuals begin practicing their selections to be "broadcast" to the group; readers concentrate on conveying the selection's meaning through expression. At this time individuals may also develop a comprehension question to pose to the group after the radio reading has finished.

The teacher or a student introduces the show, and the first broadcaster begins reading while the audience listens. The audience should not need to read along because the broadcaster (ideally) reads in an expressive manner to capture the audience and convey meaning. At the end of the show, broadcasters can ask the audience their comprehension questions.

Teacher Tips

➤ A play or real microphone can add some authenticity to this activity.

➤ Radio reading can be audio- or videotaped for future broadcast at a listening center, for example, or for home viewing!

SIMPLE STEPS: RADIO READING

1. Teachers activate prior knowledge of the reading selection topic.
2. Students read the entire selection to themselves and prepare an assigned portion to read aloud as in radio broadcast.
3. After students have had enough time to practice, the radio show is introduced, and the broadcasters read their parts while the audience listens without reading along.
4. At the end of the reading, broadcasters ask their comprehension questions.

Phrase Boundary Marking

To help students understand how to chunk words into meaningful phrases, they are given passages and asked to read to find and mark the phrase boundaries within sentences. This activity provides practice in reading with appropriate phrasing and promotes reading with expression, because the placement of the boundary marks affects the way the words are read.

Steps for Instruction

Students are given a paragraph, typed without any punctuation, and instructed to add two slash lines to indicate a long pause, as might be used for a period, and one slash to mark chunks of meaningful phrases (see Figure 5.1). Because talking has imbedded phrase boundaries, students are encouraged to read their selection aloud to help mark the boundaries. Upon completion students are encouraged to try out their interpretations, reading and rereading them. As students read their passages, they also engage in discussions about different boundary placements and how a particular placement affects fluency and understanding.

Teacher Tips

Although any written text, including written speeches, can be used to mark phrase boundaries, poetry is an appealing genre with which to introduce this activity. The work of A. A. Milne (1952) is especially delightful and interesting, because his poems do not have the predictable rhythms and rhymes of some children's poetry, forcing students to think about their task. *Lines and Squares* and *Puppy and I* are both fine examples of poems with unique rhythms.

Teachers typically group children with different fluency needs for small-group instruction. Although this is an effective strategy, some children may need the

---

The tiny sea turtle / is the last hatchling / to break out / of her leathery egg / and crawl up / the sides of a sandy nest // she is not much bigger / than a bottle cap / and would make / a good meal / for a hungry sea bird / or crab //

FIGURE 5.1. An example of phrase boundary marking. The text is from *Into the Sea* (Guiberson, 1996, p. 1).

> **SIMPLE STEPS:**
> **PHRASE BOUNDARY MARKING**
>
> 1. Students are given a typed paragraph with all punctuation removed.
> 2. Students add one slash mark to chunk meaningful phrases and two slash marks to indicate the end of a sentence.
> 3. The passages are read aloud and the various interpretations discussed.

intense support found in teacher–student paired instruction. Neurological impress and echo reading are two teacher–student paired activities described in the following section.

SUGGESTIONS FOR WORKING IN PAIRS

In the next chapter we provide detailed ideas about fluency partnering for student teams. Here we present a few general strategies that can also be useful for fluency partners.

Neurological Impress

Also known as soft voice–loud voice or supported reading, the technique of neurological impress pairs a dysfluent reader with an able reader, usually an adult. Fluency is modeled and supported as the adult reads slightly ahead of the dysfluent partner, providing instant success for the student.

Steps for Instruction

Partners sit close together so both can hear the other well. The adult reader begins reading, using a slightly loud voice. The student begins reading in a softer voice about a second or so later, thus slightly behind the first reader. The student continues to duplicate the louder reader while he or she listens carefully. When the student begins to sound confident and fluent, the adult reader softens his or her voice or may fade out completely, joining in again when support is necessary. This reading duet takes a bit of practice, but it is quite effective.

Teacher Tips

➤ Neurological impress can be used in a choral reading situation as students are practicing prosody.

➤ This technique is appropriate to use with individuals during small-group instructional time.

SIMPLE STEPS: NEUROLOGICAL IMPRESS

1. Sitting close to the child, the adult reader begins reading a passage in a slightly loud voice.
2. The student begins reading about a second after the adult.
3. The adult reader monitors the student's reading and fades in and out, as necessary.

Echo Reading

Beginning, struggling, and dysfluent readers benefit from echo reading, in which a selection is read by an adult or other more capable reader and then "echoed" by the student. It is possible for readers to focus on fluency because in hearing an accurate and fluent model, they are able to mimic the prosodic features in addition to building an understanding of the content. This activity strengthens fluency by helping students concentrate on a smooth expressive rendition of the text while building comprehension.

Steps for Instruction

In echo reading a fluent adult reads a portion of the text. After listening to the fluent model, the student rereads or "echoes" the same passage. The echo reading continues until the end of the selection. The student concludes by reading the entire selection either silently or aloud without adult support.

The fluent reader can determine how much of the selection is read before the student echoes the reading. It can range from one sentence to one paragraph to one page, with any combination in between. The amount of text is determined by how much the individual can echo read fluently—determining that amount can take trial and error. It is best to start small and work up to larger portions of text.

SIMPLE STEPS: ECHO READING

1. An adult or able reader reads a selection of text.
2. The student "echoes" the same selection immediately after the other has finished.

Teacher Tips

➢ Echo reading is a perfect strategy to use to support comprehension in content area reading.

➢ When working with small or whole groups, choral echo reading is possible.

Although it is not recommended that students work on fluency in isolation, without supportive feedback, students may enjoy trying out their fluency skills by themselves after receiving explicit fluency instruction. The following activity combines poetry, performance, and fluency practice.

A SUGGESTION FOR INDIVIDUALIZED FLUENCY LESSONS

Poetry Performances

In order to promote independent fluency practice, some teachers regularly schedule time for students to perform poems selected and practiced on their own at school and at home. These poetry performances can range from the very simple to being very elaborate with, for example, costumes, sound effects, or scenery.

Poetry is a genre that is meant to be read aloud. Its melodic quality begs for a prosodic reading. To prepare for the performance, a poem is read and reread, sometimes becoming memorized as practiced. Although some experts recommend that poetry be used infrequently to teach fluency, others agree it makes perfect sense to use poetry as part of a fluency development program.

Steps for Instruction

After the children have had some explicit fluency instruction, they are asked to use their knowledge to read poetry aloud. First the children are invited to explore the poetry selections in the collection of poetry books that is available. Each child selects a poem to practice reading fluently for a daily poetry performance.

Students are encouraged to practice both at school and at home. At school they can practice reading into tape recorders or to a friend, and at home the practice is assigned as homework. Each Monday a sign-up sheet is placed in the room. The sign-up sheet has the day and date listed with lines for three names underneath. The children use this sheet to sign up to perform their poem when they are ready. As a guideline, the poem should be read at least 20 times before students sign up to perform.

Performances occur each day when the teacher can fit them in; many teachers schedule the performances before lunch or at the end of the day. Children perform from the "author's chair" (a special chair used to read student-written stories), or by standing on a poetry platform made of a wide wooden stepstool or wood planks. The teacher keeps track of the performances to ensure that all students have a chance to perform. Those who are too shy may play a recorded poem for the audience until comfortable enough to give the performance themselves.

SIMPLE STEPS: POETRY PERFORMANCE

1. Students select a poem.
2. The selection is read and reread to practice for an expressive rendition.
3. After approximately 20 rereadings, the student signs up to read the selection to the class during a daily poetry performance.

Teacher Tips

➤ The children are encouraged to read all types of poetry. Some may read only four lines whereas others read epic-length poetry. Many children author and read their own poems; multilingual students are encouraged to read poems in other languages.

➤ Students are invited to script poems for two voices or to be read chorally. This approach can encourage shy students to perform.

➤ Staff, administrators, teachers, and parents are invited to hear the poetry performance; some teachers organize poetry teas so that parents can attend.

Reading with Recorded Models

Using audiotapes for support is one of the earliest techniques for developing fluency (Chomsky, 1976). Students listen to taped readings of books as models and then practice along with the tape. They also can practice with partners and parents until they are able to read a passage or a page fluently. They can then perform for a partner, teacher, or class, or they can tape their own rendition, which can be filed with a copy of the passage for the class. This method allows students to listen to themselves and develop a metacognitive awareness of their own fluency strengths and weaknesses so that they can develop personal fluency goals.

Teacher Tips

➤ Many tapes of books are recorded at too fast a speed for struggling readers, so you may want to invest in tape recorders with speed controls for the classroom. These are quite inexpensive and allow you, or the students, to select a setting that is reasonable for young readers.

➤ Older children can record whole books for younger readers. In this way they get practice, and the primary classrooms get a set of tapes and books for their use.

RESOURCES FOR FLUENCY PRACTICE

A large variety of book selections is appropriate for fluency development. We suggest using the books that the students seem to enjoy the most, along with songs and poems. In addition, carefully chosen pages or paragraphs from chapter books can create an excitement for fluency activities with older children.

Children's Magazines

Both narrative and expository passages are available for fluency development in children's magazines. The titles and publishers include *Kids Discover*, published by Kids Discover; *Ranger Rick*, published by the Federal Wildlife Federation; *National Geographic for Kids*, published by National Geographic; and *Ladybug, Cricket, Muse*, and others, published by Cricket. Children's weekly news magazines, *Weekly Reader* (published by WRC Media) and *Time for Kids* (published by Time Inc.) also include passages appropriate for fluency lessons.

Readers' Theatre

Readers' Theatre sources can be found in both published books and on the Internet. Speeches are available at www.edchange.org/multicultural/speeches. Two websites for Readers' Theatre information and scripts are www.aaronshep.com and www.loiswalker.com. Sources for published scripts include Readers' Theatre books by Win Braun and Carl Braun or Helen Raczuk and Marilyn Smith (both available from Portage and Main Press, Calgary, Alberta, Canada; 800-667-9673).

Poetry

Paul Fleischman has written a number of books of poetry that are wonderful for fluency practice: *Joyful Noise: Poems for Two Voices* (winner of the 1989 Newberry Medal), *I Am a Phoenix: Poems for Two Voices*, and *Big Talk: Poems for Four Voices* are a must for every classroom library.

Teacher Professional Development

Martinez, M., Roser, N. L., & Strecker, S. (1998/1999). "I never thought I could be a star": A Readers' Theatre ticket to fluency. *Reading Teacher, 52*, 326–334.

Opitz, M. F., Rasinski, T. V., & Bird, L. B. (1998). *Goodbye round robin reading: Twenty-five effective oral reading strategies.* Portsmouth, NH: Heinemann.

Rasinski, T. V. (2004). Creating fluent readers. *Educational Leadership, 61*, 46–51.

DON'T STOP HERE

No doubt you have found something that you are ready to try with your students. Keep reading! There are more activities to be found in Chapter 6.

STUDENT PARTNERS FOR FLUENCY DEVELOPMENT

Typically teaching is defined as leading to knowledge or understanding. Some teachers facilitate understanding by imparting knowledge, but exemplary teaching involves much more; it involves the ability to help students discover how to learn in a child-centered environment wherein the teacher is also a facilitator who develops learning opportunities for students. Students are supported in pursuing their interests, and they are expected to assume responsibility for managing their behaviors and evaluating their learning.

The consequences of embracing a format of student-centered learning in classrooms are staggering. The children are self-assured, self-efficacious, independent, supportive of each other, motivated, and interested. Most importantly, though, they *learn*, and they learned more than they could ever be taught through lectures or worksheets. With such positive outcomes, it makes sense to investigate ways in which fluency development can become more student-centered. Partnering students is one way.

STUDENT PARTNERS AND LEARNING

Learning is the goal of any educational experience. Covey (1989) believes that paired work helps participants learn more, become excited about the task, and gain insights that increase learning momentum. These insights, in turn, lead to further learning, excitement, and more insights.

Koskinen and Blum (1986) observed student partners working in pairs on repeated reading for fluency development. They wrote about students' enjoyment and confidence due to working together in pairs. Although enjoyment and confidence are important, there are other reasons why working in pairs benefits students. Dewey (1916/1944) discussed practices related to the social aspects of learning and noted that a social learning environment allows for student interest, responsibility, and a connection to others and their learning. This active learning creates an emotional and motivational connection to what is being learned, thus facilitating learning. Working with a partner allows for an emotional connection to the other and to the learning, which enhances motivation and a desire to learn more.

When pairing students for learning, many teachers choose to partner more capable with less capable students, believing that this combination is necessary to support the learning of the less able child. Rogoff (1990), along with Forman and Cazden (1994), describe models in which novice pairs, or two less capable children, engage in learning. The first, Rogoff's model, describes learning between peer partners who are at the same level of understanding or inexperience. Here peers serve as resources for each other through social interactions and task completion. In the second model, presented by Forman and Cazden, one child acts as the support person who watches, listens, helps, directs, and corrects the partner, who completes the activity. The learning occurs as the pair exchange their roles, offering information, giving and following directions, and asking questions.

As previously noted in Chapter 2, further evidence in support of pairing students who may be at the same level of ability or lack of understanding comes from Piaget (Rogoff, 1990), who explained that paired students come to a task as equals, and in talking together they are able to restructure their thinking, based on the other's point of view and logic. When working with a peer, both children learn as they try to resolve differences of opinion, conflicts, and support each other's learning. The same kind of learning does not seem to occur with an adult–child pairing because there is an unequal balance of power (Rogoff, 1990; King-Sears & Carpenter, 1997). In addition, Piaget believes that children treat situations in a different way when they, not the adult, are in charge (Rogoff, 1990). Children in charge tend to be more playful and exploratory in their learning, but also less goal oriented. To help children become more goal oriented, they should be required to set their own goals as part of the paired learning process.

SELF-MANAGED REPEATED READING FOR FLUENCY DEVELOPMENT

The clinical model of repeated reading is implemented in a one-on-one format. The adult follows along as a child reads, supports the child afterward, and then the child immediately rereads, resulting in fluency improvement. It is clear that this activity helps develop fluency, but how many teachers truly have time to implement one-on-one instruction daily with dysfluent readers? We didn't! Student self-managed repeated reading (SMRR) is one answer; teachers whose students have been involved in this activity have been pleased with the results.

Dysfluent students involved in SMRR follow a unique path in becoming fluent readers. They learn and work together to integrate all the characteristics of fluent reading while rereading and discussing passages. They become responsible for supporting each other, maintaining their records of improvement, setting goals, and looking after the fluency materials. Once the students are trained in these skills, the teacher does little other than checking on task behavior and progress.

A study of SMRR groups (Moskal, 2002) indicates that the progress toward fluency is a result of several factors. First, students involved in self-managed activities were in charge of their improvement, and the motivation derived from being in charge, along with the collaboration of peers, seemed to facilitate growth. Interestingly, students who were less able to stay focused during SMRR still improved their fluency rates. This is a common phenomenon with student-managed learning: Students tend to improve even if their management skills are less than proficient (McDougall & Brady, 1998). Second, students credited themselves for the improvement. Most all students involved in SMRR felt responsible for their own and their partner's growth, thus making the activity personally significant and important. Next, those who had few opportunities to shine in other academic areas naturally played leadership roles in the peer dyads. The students saw themselves as teachers while they carefully recorded miscues and supported their partner between readings. Finally, students documented tangible evidence of their fluency growth on record sheets; these sheets made it clear that they were becoming fluent.

CHOOSING STUDENTS FOR SELF-MANAGED REPEATED READING

SMRR seems to work best for those children whose fluency development needs a boost. In other words, students who are below or at the low end of the average words-correct-per-minute rate range for their grade level or need assistance in prosody could benefit from the activity. Teachers use different criteria to select students for SMRR, but all have considered the following: (1) rate, fluency scale scores, and comprehension scores from the classroom fluency snapshot (CFS); (2) an inability to read familiar texts smoothly and effortlessly (Schreiber, 1980); and (3) the ability to read with some basic skills. Let's briefly look at the process Mrs. Burns went through in January to select students in her second-grade class for SMRR.

Mrs. Burns preselected approximately 15 students who she felt needed fluency work based on her literacy assessments, observations, and the January CFS (see Table 6.1). Mrs. Burns discussed the selections with her instructional aide, focusing on the

TABLE 6.1. Mrs. Burns's January Classroom Fluency Snapshot

wcpm range	wcpm rates of students in the class not selected for SMRR	wcpm rates of students considered for SMRR	wcpm rates of students selected for SMRR
140	138		
135			
130			
125			
120			
115			
110	107		Kenny, 110
100			
95			
90			
85	83		
80		78	
75		76	
70		69	Stephie, 70
65		67	Bobby, 65
60		61, 63	Katy, 63
55			
50		47, 51	
45		45	
40		38, 39	
35			
30	30		
25	24		

Note. English language learners were not given this assessment. The average words-correct-per-minute range for second grade is 60–90.

students' strengths, needs, and how the behaviors of each might or might not affect progress in a self-managed learning situation. Mrs. Burns finally chose four students who needed fluency work but who were also, she thought, "able to work on their own." Mrs. Burns saw great potential in these students. With the additional responsibility of self-managed learning, she hoped to build motivation and a feeling of accomplishment that would spill over into the rest of their schooling experience.

Mrs. Burns chose Stephie, Katy, Bobby, and Kenny. Stephie was considered a below-average reader; she had attended the school's resource reading program in first grade. She missed being included in that program in second grade by 1 assessment point. Mrs. Burns described Stephie not as falling through the cracks—she was *stuck in* the crack.

Katy, an above-average reader, was bilingual. Her oral reading was choppy, and it was felt that she just needed a little extra support. She was an interpersonal learner who had an understanding of how reading should sound. Although her reading was dysfluent, it was usually expressive.

Bobby was an average reader and had just "graduated" from the resource reading program. Although he had made considerable gains in that program, he simply was not a fluent reader. Kenny was a strong reader, but he too wasn't fluent. He was unable to chunk text into appropriate phrases, and his reading sounded choppy due to self-imposed pauses to clear his throat or take a breath. Kenny was selected because Mrs. Burns knew he would improve, even though he could be shy in group activities.

TEACHER PREPARATION AND IMPLEMENTATION OF SELF-MANAGED REPEATED READING

In the SMRR activity, dysfluent readers learn the characteristics of fluency: appropriate rate, accuracy, and prosody. They read and listen to each other, manage a modified miscue analysis, support their partners, record their progress, self-assess, and set fluency goals for rereading. They also learn to use a calculator and stopwatch to compute a words-correct-per-minute rate. Modeling and training for SMRR takes an initial time commitment from the teacher, but after that, the children become self-sufficient.

Materials

The management of materials in the SMRR is quite simple. Before starting, it is necessary to consider what materials are needed and where they will be kept in the classroom. Materials that seem to work best include:

➢ One plastic 9″ × 11″ envelope or file with a string clasp.

➢ Two different colored pencils for each child.

➢ Record and passage sheets.

➢ Sharpened pencils.

➢ A container to hold the individual plastic envelopes (we used a magazine holder).

➢ A file or envelope for the completed work.

Each child kept two sharpened pencils, two colored pencils, and record sheets in his or her envelope. Typed copies of the passages were kept in either a separate folder or the individual's plastic envelope. Other materials included:

➢ One stopwatch per pair.

➢ One calculator per pair.

➢ A container for the stopwatches and calculators.

In learning to self-manage, students learn to prepare for the session and clean up after they are done. These behaviors are incorporated into the process of learning the repeated-reading activity.

Teachers Prepare to Help Students Manage Learning Themselves

In developing self-managed behaviors, students become actively involved in learning and practicing strategies to develop oral reading fluency while increasing their interest, motivation, and sense of empowerment (Johnson, 1998). To foster these qualities and ensure that the behaviors become part of a routine, students need to practice self-management skills frequently. This means it is best for the teacher to engage the children daily in modeling and training in SMRR.

A model suggested by Johnson, Graham, and Harris (1997) appears to work well in helping students understand the process in which they will engage to develop self-managed learning and fluency strategy use. The steps of the Johnson et al. model included here are (1) preskill development, (2) conferencing, (3) discussing the strategy, (4) modeling, (5) collaborative practice, and (6) independent practice.

First, in *preskill development*, students are told what they are going to do and that the ultimate goal is fluent oral reading. *Group conferences* are held to *discuss the repeated reading strategy* and its connection to fluency development. Repeated reading and its use as a strategy are emphasized, and the children are encouraged to talk about and use the word *strategy. Modeling* of repeated reading and the self-managed learning process is followed by *collaborative practice* with student pairs and the teacher. In the final step, *independent practice*, the student pairs work on the repeated reading strategy without the teacher's support.

An Example from Mrs. Burns

Using the six steps suggested by Johnson et al. (1997), Mrs. Burns divided the SMRR training into three phases: (1) modeling, (2) guided practice, and (3) independent practice. In the daily modeling phase of 30- to 45-minute time blocks, *preskill development* was cultivated as the group discussed fluency, self-management, and repeated reading. Students talked about their concepts of fluency, and Mrs. Burns stressed the goal of the activity as being fluent reading. In addition, students were asked to share why they thought they had been chosen for such an interesting activity. All understood that there was an aspect of fluency at which they could improve. There were daily *group conferences* covering repeated reading and self-management techniques. It was vitally important for the children to understand why they were involved and what the outcome was expected to be. *Discussions* led to that end.

The training and modeling continued as the four students were walked through the procedures they would be following. First the students each took a turn reading and then rereading a passage aloud. A discussion followed, focused on the changes from the first to the second reading. Next they were given a copy of a passage while Bobby read aloud. The others practiced following along, marking the miscues made by Bobby, and providing positive, supportive feedback. The untimed record sheet (see Form 6.1) was then introduced, and Bobby filled it out in front of the group, based on his evaluation of his reading and the group's input. The students then *collaboratively practiced* the repeated reading procedures with a partner and Mrs. Burns's support. Finally the students learned to use the stopwatches and calculators to calculate a words-correct-per-minute rate for the timed repeated readings held once a week (on Fridays). After 5 days of modeling, the students began the guided practice phase. For an overview of the steps, see Table 6.2.

The 30- to 45-minute daily sessions continued during the guided practice phase. Mrs. Burns explained to the children that she was changing her role: She was now there to watch and help rather than teach. If the children asked for help, they would receive it. If Mrs. Burns saw something wrong, she would wait as long as she possibly could without saying something in hopes the children would correct the error themselves. If they didn't, she would intervene. This phase lasted for 4 days.

FORM 6.1. REPEATED READING RECORD SHEET

Name _____ Date _____

Title _____ Start Page _____ End Page _____

· ·

First Reading

How do you think you read?
Is there a place where your partner can help you?
Did you understand what you read? (If not, can your partner help?)

	Always		Sometimes		Never
I used the punctuation correctly.	5	4	3	2	1
I read with expression.	5	4	3	2	1
I was able to read smoothly without pausing a lot.	5	4	3	2	1
The reading sounded like talking.	5	4	3	2	1

Number of Miscues _____ Goal for next reading _____ (or circle one above)

· ·

Second Reading

How do you think you read?
Is there a place where your partner can help you?
Did you understand what you read? (If not, can your partner help?)

	Always		Sometimes		Never
I used the punctuation correctly.	5	4	3	2	1
I read with expression.	5	4	3	2	1
I was able to read smoothly without pausing a lot.	5	4	3	2	1
The reading sounded like talking.	5	4	3	2	1

Number of Miscues _____

I was able to reach my goal.   Yes   No

My goal for tomorrow's reading is _____

TABLE 6.2. Steps for Self-Managed Repeated Reading

1. Choose student participants based on assessments and teacher-selected criteria.

2. Gather materials and decide where to store them so students can access them easily.

3. Model the repeated reading procedure and self-managed behaviors. Include preskill development, conferencing, and discussions. Walk students through the procedures to gather and clean up the materials.

4. Students engage in guided practice. In this step they practice SMRR with support provided by the teacher when necessary.

5. Independent practice begins when students are able to continue the SMRR activity on their own.

After 9 days of modeling and guided practice, the students were ready to work independently. They began the session by gathering the materials they needed and bringing them to their work place. They removed the record sheet and corresponding typed copy of the passage they were reading for that day from a plastic folder. Students took the colored pencils for recording miscues and checked a list to determine their partner for the day, working with different partners on each successive day.

The repeated reading activity began when the partners decided who would read first. The reader began and the listener followed along on the typed copy, circling any miscues to be shared with the reader in colored pencil. When each oral reading was completed, the listener referred to the questions on the record sheet to (1) ask for the reader's assessment of the reading, (2) check if he or she could assist with any trouble spots, and (3) check for understanding. The partners discussed what was done well and what needed improvement in terms of overall fluency. The reader filled out the record sheet with input from the listener, noting the number of miscues, a goal for the next reading, and the reader's fluency self-assessment (use a Likert scale). The process was then repeated once, with a different colored pencil used to circle the miscues, for a total of two readings.

Next the partners switched roles: The listener became the reader, and the reader became the listener. The same procedure was repeated with the roles reversed, as the "new" reader began the first of the two readings.

When the partners had both read their passages twice and filled out the record sheet, materials were placed in a box and everything was put away. Once a week on Friday, the partners used stopwatches to time the readings and calculate a words-correct-per-minute rate. A different but similar record sheet was used for this process (see Form 6.2).

FORM 6.2. TIMED REPEATED READING RECORD SHEET

Name _____ Date _____

Title _____ Level _____

Start Page _____ End Page _____ Number of Words _____

....

First Reading

Number of Miscues _____ Number of Seconds _____

_____ words − _____ miscues = ____ ÷ 60 = _____ wcpm

_____ correct words read in 1 minute

	Always		Sometimes		Never
I used the punctuation correctly.	5	4	3	2	1
I read with expression.	5	4	3	2	1
I was able to group words that went together.	5	4	3	2	1
The reading sounded good.	5	4	3	2	1

WCPM goal for the next reading _____

....

Second Reading

Number of Miscues ____ Number of Seconds _

_____ words − _____ miscues = ____ ÷ 60 = _____ wcpm

_____ correct words read in 1 minute

	Always		Sometimes		Never
I used the punctuation correctly.	5	4	3	2	1
I read with expression.	5	4	3	2	1
I was able to group words that went together.	5	4	3	2	1
The reading sounded good.	5	4	3	2	1

Did you reach your goal? Yes No   WCPM goal for the next reading _____

Passage Selection for Independent Repeated Reading

Because students work independently on the SMRR, passages need to be at an independent reading level. It is at this level that students are able to read the text with some ease and record the miscues of partners, which enables them to provide feedback for improving fluency. Because materials categorized as independent are read with ease, a high degree of accuracy is maintained. One way to ensure that passages are at the correct level is to use texts that are read and used for strategy instruction during guided or instructional reading time. Mrs. Burns used familiar texts of approximately 100 words that had been read in an instructional setting the week prior. Her students needed no word recognition assistance from her while working on the SMRR. Any support the children needed was available from one of the students working on the SMRR.

FLUENCY DEVELOPMENT AS A RESULT OF THE SELF-MANAGED REPEATED READING

Mrs. Burns's four students engaged in SMRR daily from January through May, at which time they were assessed with another CFS. Simmons and Kame'enui (1999) suggest that second-grade students increase their reading rates approximately five

Student pairs work to improve fluency using student self-managed repeated reading.

words correct per minute each month of second grade; therefore, we might expect a 5-month gain of 25 words correct per minute from the SMRR group. The results of the CFS showed an increase in their reading rate by an average of 29.8 words correct per minute, practically a 6-month gain in 5 months! Interestingly, a comparison group increased their reading rate by only 16.2 words correct per minute during the same time frame.

The quality of the students' reading fluency also improved, as measured by the Multidimensional Fluency Scale (Zutell & Rasinski, 1991). During the last weeks of May, all four children scored their highest ratings not only on the rereading, but more importantly, on the first reading of a passage. Students were able to self-assess, set goals, and focus on various fluency characteristics; as a result they were able to read smoothly, accurately, and with expression. In addition, Mrs. Burns found that the students became highly successful at self-management; they became self-sufficient and able to engage in the SMRR activity without any outside assistance. In other words, they did it entirely on their own! There was only one day—the last day they were scheduled to work through SMRR—that they got into trouble. They were being so silly that Mrs. Burns had to stop the session early.

In an interview Mrs. Burns noted that the children were very invested in their work. She said, "Bobby would come in and say, 'Whoa, we've gotta get down to work.' And those two boys, especially for little second-grade boys, were very, very focused. Katy was also very focused. Stephie did okay." But something happened that made Mrs. Burns think this activity was special. She observed good things happening other than an improvement in fluency. "[It's] what I noticed the most," she smiled, "an increase in their confidence level." What a wonderful side effect!

A TWIST ON SELF-MANAGED REPEATED READING: THE FLUENCY EXPERTS

Judy, the third-grade teacher introduced earlier, also used the SMRR activity in her classroom. Ten children were chosen to participate, but Judy didn't train them all. Two boys, known as the "fluency experts," were trained in SMRR and expected to train the other eight students. These two boys lacked confidence and scored in the bottom quarter of the CFS continuum. The boys were trained following the same procedures used with Mrs. Burns's class. With help, the boys presented the SMRR to their classmates, organized the modeling and guided reading practice sessions, and were available to assist, when needed. As a result, a tremendous increase in confidence was observed in the fluency experts—who, by the way, also improved their fluency.

Another twist in Judy's version of SMRR was that instead of marking miscues on a typed copy of the selected passage, the third-grade partners read directly from their guided reading texts and marked any miscues with Post-it arrows. The arrows, kept inside their fluency folders, were used over and over. This method proved to be beneficial because it saved time and paper. In addition, the children were able to select the 100-word passage on the spot, whereas before, the selections, although made by the students, were made a week ahead of time, and the same passage was read by everyone.

IMPLICATIONS FOR IMPLEMENTATION

When planning to implement the SMRR with dysfluent student pairs, it is wise to consider the following:

> Teachers should allot the amount of time necessary to model the procedures as well as prepare the typed passages for the listening partners to mark miscues. The modeling time is necessary each year with a new group of students, whereas the time needed to type passages diminishes as a file of passages builds from previous years.

> Teachers should be careful not to emphasize rate or speed too much.

> Passage selection for independent fluency development is important, especially for dysfluent partners. The use of text previously read and reread in an instructional setting will almost guarantee that the readers in SMRR find success in working toward fluency.

> It's best for the students to have some kind of accountability for their fluency progress, such as record sheets (already described) or even audio recordings of the SMRR sessions.

> Teachers need to consider how many repeated reading sessions to implement for a particular passage. There aren't set rules, so it's best to keep the goals for fluency in mind. To keep the organization as simple as possible, the children in Mrs. Burns's class chose passages to reread for a week at a time. Monday through Thursday the passage was read twice each day, and on Friday the two readings were timed to calculate a words-correct-per-minute rate. A new passage was then used the following Monday.

In Judy's room the children were able to select the passage from the book they were using for guided reading. Judy knew reading practice was important, so she let them choose the passage to increase their motivation to read. The only stipulations were that (1) the material selected had been covered during guided reading; (2) the passage chosen was 100–150 words, or approximately 10–15 lines of text; (3) the reading partner and the listening partner had the same book; and (4) the reading partner showed the listening partner exactly where the reading would begin and end. Many pairs marked off the beginning and end with the Post-it arrows.

➤ We have strong positive feelings about including student choice in learning. However, when it comes to choosing partners for SMRR, we highly recommend that the teacher set up a schedule whereby partners rotate daily. This rotation precludes hurt feelings and time wasted in discussing who works with whom. With a schedule, the children know they eventually will work with the partner of their choice.

THE BENEFITS OF STUDENT SELF-MANAGED REPEATED READING

There are advantages in using paired and self-managed learning for children who are equally dysfluent. First, SMRR creates a sense of self-efficacy as the students begin to understand fluency more fully and realize that rate is just one component. Improved scores on the Multidimensional Fluency Scale and student-selected fluency goals show this progress clearly. At first, most students set tangible goals. Rate and accuracy are easy to measure and easy to understand. With practice and confidence, students set goals that are more "squishy" (as one student put it) or more subjective. Smoothness, appropriate phrasing, and expressiveness become the common choices as the students gain fluency and understanding of fluency components.

Second, the SMRR programs create a sense of community learning and collaboration. The SMRR is a natural extension for a community of collaborative learners, each with strengths and the ability to improve. Of course, SMRR programs look slightly different for individual teachers within their own community cultures.

Finally, the SMRR program is a viable strategy for fluency development, even if some students need support working independently. Four second-grade boys engaged in SMRR. Their fluency rates improved considerably even though the teacher needed to remind them to work together appropriately. In retrospect, the teacher realized these boys would have behaved better in a one-on-one format with an adult.

A LOOK TO CHAPTER 7

As noted above, although SMRR works well to develop fluent reading, there may be children for whom a one-on-one situation is optimal. The next chapter describes a volunteer program in which community members tutored dysfluent readers one-on-one in the classroom.

CHAPTER 7

VOLUNTEER PARTNERS FOR FLUENCY DEVELOPMENT

I t is well known that the clinical one-on-one repeated reading model is an exceptional strategy for improving the fluency of readers. Unfortunately, some school districts may not be able to implement the one-on-one model because they do not have reading specialists, and those that do have reading specialists may not be able to support dysfluent readers on the specialist's case load.

THE VOLUNTEER PARTNER PROGRAM

In a school district located north of Chicago, teachers were in the second year of a professional development collaboration, called Everybody Reads, with National-Louis University. In Everybody Reads university professors and facilitators, including us, worked alongside teachers to investigate how fluency instruction could improve student performance. The teachers supported their students by integrating fluency instruction into the curriculum and paid close attention to those who were in need of an extra fluency boost. Many of these children had just "graduated" from or did not qualify, for the district's pull-out reading support system but still needed literacy guidance, especially in fluency. Understanding the benefits of the repeated reading procedure the university and teacher participants of Everybody Reads developed a program to train community volunteers to implement the one-on-one repeated reading model with children who could benefit from the focused assistance.

A parent volunteer coordinated the program for the schools in the district. Meetings were held with the university team, the district reading coordinator, and the participating teachers to outline the necessary components of the volunteer program. The components included (1) recruiting the volunteers, (2) training the volunteers, (3) implementing the program, and (4) mentoring the volunteers.

Teachers, with guidance from the district's literacy coordinator and the university team, brainstormed how the volunteer program might work. It was felt that the program needed to be simple, consistent, and allow for easy record keeping and communication between the teacher and the volunteer, even if the teacher was in the middle of instruction when the volunteer arrived. Volunteers would need to be trained so that they understood the components of fluency, the repeated reading activity, when the book selection was too difficult for a child, and when sufficient progress had been made so that a child could begin working with more difficult reading materials (Blachowicz et al., 2006).

In the plan participating teachers would be assigned a minimum of two volunteers, each visiting the class at least once during the week on different days. This system seemed the best way to accommodate the fact that many volunteers wanted to participate but could only devote 1 day a week to the program. Each participating student, then, would work twice a week with one of the teacher's assigned volunteers. These volunteers would work individually with several students who had been identified by their teachers as dysfluent readers or as those who could benefit from fluency support. Once in the classroom, volunteers would refer to a binder, called the "tutor's notebook," that included all the necessary records and materials to implement the fluency intervention. This same binder would include sections for record keeping and communication between the volunteer and the teacher, and it would allow the different volunteers to work with some of the same children. For example, a tutor visiting the classroom on a Thursday could refer to the notes made by the volunteer who worked with the same children on Tuesday. With the plan in place, it was time to recruit volunteers.

Recruiting Volunteers

The parent coordinator recruited volunteers from two major neighborhood groups: the district's parent organization and the community of senior citizens. Letters were sent (see Figure 7.1 for a sample) and visits were made. When visiting groups to solicit volunteers, the coordinator passed out flyers (see Figure 7.2 for a sample) and gave a short address that included:

Dear parents, guardians, and other family and community members,

Our school district is working on an exciting project called Everybody Reads. The goal of this project is to develop models for oral reading fluency instruction in our schools.

This year we are working on individual tutoring models. For this we need volunteers who can donate 1½ hours once a week or 1 hour twice a week to work with students. Tutors will be trained to work one-to-one with the children.

A tutoring session with a single child will last 15-20 minutes, during which the student will practice reading materials supplied by the teacher. The tutor will listen, encourage, and help record student progress.

If you enjoy working with children and could make a regular commitment to tutoring, please contact the teacher who sent this letter or Sandy Johnson, volunteer coordinator. The 2-hour training session will take place the week of October 15th.

We hope to hear from you!

Sincerely,

Sandy Johnson, Volunteer Coordinator
Phone and e-mail address:
Classroom teacher name and phone contact:

FIGURE 7.1. Sample letter to recruit volunteers.

➤ A brief description of the volunteer program and its purpose.

➤ A brief description of the repeated reading process.

➤ The rewards from watching students progress over an extended period of time.

➤ The rewards from contributing to the community school.

➤ The rewards from making a real difference in a child's reading development.

The groups learned that a 2-hour training session would be provided and that they would need to make a commitment of 1–1½ hours weekly, October through May.

VOLUNTEERS NEEDED
FOR
READING TUTORING

WITH: Four students in grades 1–3
WHEN: Once a week for 1½ hours, October–May
WHERE: Your "home" elementary school

Many parents and community members worked last year with teachers in your school to tutor children in reading fluency. As teachers continue this program, and as more teachers become interested in trying it, more volunteers are needed. If you enjoy working with children and would like to hear more about this opportunity, contact: [name, phone, e-mail]

FIGURE 7.2. Flyer to recruit volunteers.

They would work one-on-one with each student and remain partnered with the same teacher throughout the year.

The parent coordinator was pleased to have little trouble finding the number of volunteers necessary. In order to participate, the volunteers needed to commit to visiting their assigned classes once a week. It was decided that volunteer parents would work in their neighborhood school, but not in the classes of their own children. Volunteers were then sent invitations to attend a training session to be held in the district office before beginning to work with the students (see Figure 7.3 for a sample).

The Training Session

The volunteers assembled one morning for the fluency training session. Coffee and rolls were available while administrators, teachers, and volunteers got to know each other. The training session began with formal introductions and a brief overview of good reading and good readers. Participants were shown a copy of the good reader chart (see Figure 1.1, p. 8), and it was explained that good readers have print knowledge, prior knowledge, vocabulary knowledge, and comprehension, all integrated with fluent reading that is well paced, well phrased, expressive, and accurate. Participants were told that good readers are motivated to read and that this motivation drives them to read more and become even better readers.

```
Dear Everybody Reads volunteers,

    Thank you for your interest in working with a child
as part of the Everybody Reads program. A tutor train-
ing will be held on Thursday morning, October 5, from 9
to 11 at the Administration Building, 1234 School
Avenue. You will hear an overview of the program and
see a demonstration of the specific teaching strategy
you will be using with your students.
    If you haven't done so already, please arrange, with
your classroom teacher, a time to meet weekly with the
students.
    Once again, thank you for your generosity. We are
anticipating an exciting and rewarding year! Feel free
to contact me if you have any questions or if you can't
come to the meeting.

    Sincerely,

    Sandy Johnson, Volunteer Coordinator
    Phone and e-mail address:
```

FIGURE 7.3. Sample invitation to the training session.

Volunteers next learned that fluency development was the focus of their work because the ability to read fluently is highly correlated with other areas of reading aptitude. The repeated reading of a passage, along with support between those readings, is considered by experts to be a highly successful method for developing fluency. It was explained that the purpose of the volunteer program was to supply practice in reading fluently, provide the students with a positive reading experience, increase reading self-esteem, and record progress that the students could see and understand. The HoPE diagram (see Figure 7.4) showed the guiding principles for fluency development: Students need to _hear good reading models_, _practice reading_ high interest _materials on the appropriate level_, and _evaluate_ their _progress_. This evaluation comes in the form of both adult monitoring and student self-assessment.

The timed repeated reading strategy to be used with the children for fluency development was outlined for the volunteers. They were told that during one session their students would read the same passage of approximately 100 words three times while they took a modified running record of the miscues and amount of

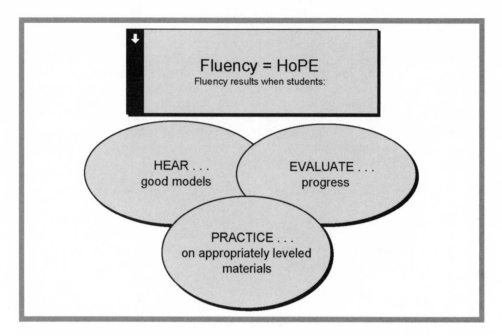

FIGURE 7.4. HoPE: Guiding principles for fluency development.

time taken to read. The expectation, of course, was that the child would increase rate and decrease miscues with each successive reading. In addition, it was pointed out that the process should be enjoyable for both student and volunteer.

At this time in the training session the volunteers viewed a videotape of the repeated reading process being implemented. The video was not professionally made, although it was recorded in a university media center for quality sound and picture. (During the first year of the program, an additional video was made, of a volunteer implementing the repeated reading strategy with a student, and used in subsequent training sessions.) Before viewing the video, volunteers were told to observe the tutor's easygoing manner and the student's level of comfort.

After discussing the video, each participant received a volunteer packet that included sample materials. Those in attendance learned that all sheets and materials needed for implementing the repeated readings would be available in the tutor's notebook located in each classroom. Next the meeting facilitators went through the volunteer packet. The handouts that were included in the volunteer packet are described below.

Basic Process for Timed Repeated Readings

This handout contained the instructional process volunteers would use with their students (see Table 7.1). The list of necessary materials was reviewed. Reading levels of students were predetermined, so volunteers simply needed to consult a list of leveled books (described later) and choose the appropriate level and passage for repeated reading. Typical oral reading rates were provided as a guide and to ensure that tutors did not select overly difficult material. As a guide, tutors were told that the texts selected for repeated reading should be relatively easy for the child, with no more that 15 errors on the first reading.

Sample Fluency Record Sheet

Participants received both a blank and completed fluency record sheet (see Form 7.1 and Figure 7.5). This was the same sheet that was used to model the repeated reading process in the video presentation. Record keeping in the top section of the sheet was reviewed as well as the calculation of a words-correct-per-minute rate. The students are instructed to self-assess their *correct use of punctuation* and *read with expression* for each reading by rating themselves on the 5-point scale. This self-assessment helps students become aware of the components of fluent reading.

The meeting facilitator next explained that the third rereading during the repeated reading session could be untimed to allow students to concentrate on reading with expression. If this were the choice, a words-correct-per-minute rate would not be calculated.

Fluency Graphs

To highlight an increase in rate and decrease in miscues over the readings, the adult–student pairs fill out a fluency graph. This graph is given to the students after the session to take home. Both a prepared graph corresponding to the fluency record sheet and two blank forms are included in the volunteer packet (see Figure 7.6 and Forms 7.2 and 7.3).

At this point in the presentation, a video clip was shown of a tutor filling out the fluency record sheet and fluency graph after the third rereading of a text. Volunteers were asked to pay attention to (1) the interaction between the tutor and the student, (2) the brief discussion of miscues made after the reading, (3) the sharing of the calculator to determine the words-correct-per-minute rate, (4) the student self-assessment, and (5) the graphing of miscues and the words-correct-per-minute rate on the fluency graph.

text continues on page 106

TABLE 7.1. The Basic Process for Timed Repeated Readings

You will need:

- A book at the student's level.
- A stopwatch or watch with a second hand.
- A pencil.
- A calculator.
- Two crayons or colored pencils or markers.
- Fluency record sheet.
- Fluency graph sheet.

1. Consult the guide to determine how many words are in the passage *or* count the number of words that the student is to read.
2. Explain to the student that you are going to work together to help him or her become a better reader. You will do this by practicing the reading of a passage three times. Ask the student to think about the reading beforehand by reading the title together. Briefly discuss.
3. The student begins reading the passage for the first time. Immediately, you begin timing. *During* the reading, note miscues by making tally marks or writing the words on a sheet of paper. (Miscues include words that are read incorrectly, as well as words that you may have to tell the student.) *Following* the reading, jot down how many seconds it lasted.
4. Have the fluency record sheet handy. With the student, determine the words correct per minute, using the formula indicated. Depending on the student, you may wish to have him or her use the calculator, or you may choose to do the calculating yourself. The student should self-assess the reading along the scale. Graph the results from the reading. Graph the errors in one color and the words correct per minute in the other color.
5. The student rereads the passage, and you document the results two more times.
6. Discuss the improved performance as well some goals for the next meeting.

Typical oral reading rate ranges

Grade level	Oral reading rates
1	30–70
2	60–90
3	80–120
4	100–130
5	120–150

FORM 7.1. FLUENCY RECORD SHEET

Child's Name _____ Date _____

Book Title _____ Level _____

Start Page _____ End Page _____ Number of Words _____

Tutor's Name _____

....

First Reading

Number of Seconds _____ Number of Micues _____

_____ words − _____ miscues = _____ correct words ÷ _____ seconds × 60 = _____ wcpm

(100 words − 5 miscues = 95 correct words ÷ 120 seconds × 60 = 48 words correct per minute)

	Always				Rarely
Correct use of punctuation	5	4	3	2	1
Read with expression	5	4	3	2	1

....

Second Reading

Number of Seconds _____ Number of Micues _____

_____ words − _____ miscues = _____ correct words ÷ _____ seconds × 60 = _____ wcpm

	Always				Rarely
Correct use of punctuation	5	4	3	2	1
Read with expression	5	4	3	2	1

....

Third Reading

Number of Seconds _____ Number of Micues _____

_____ words − _____ miscues = _____ correct words ÷ _____ seconds × 60 = _____ wcpm

	Always				Rarely
Correct use of punctuation	5	4	3	2	1
Read with expression	5	4	3	2	1

Child's Name _____ Date _____

Book Title This is the Bear _____ Level _____

Start Page _1_____ End Page _7_____ Number of words 122_____

Tutor's Name MK Moskal _____

. . . .

First Reading

Number of Seconds 125_____ Number of Micues 9_____

122 words – _9_ miscues = 113 correct words ÷ 125 seconds × 60 = 54_ wcpm

(100 words – 5 miscues = 95 correct words ÷ 120 seconds × 60 = 48 words correct per minute)

	Always			Rarely	
Correct use of punctuation	5	4	③	2	1
Read with expression	5	4	③	2	1

. . . .

Second Reading

Number of Seconds 111_____ Number of Micues 0_____

122 words – _0_ miscues = 122 correct words ÷ 111 seconds × 60 = _5_ wcpm

	Always			Rarely	
Correct use of punctuation	5	④	3	2	1
Read with expression	5	4	③	2	1

. . . .

Third Reading

Number of Seconds 90_____ Number of Micues 0_____

122 words – _0_ miscues = 122 correct words ÷ 90_ seconds × 60 = 81_ wcpm

	Always			Rarely	
Correct use of punctuation	5	④	3	2	1
Read with expression	5	④	3	2	1

FIGURE 7.5. Example of a completed fluency record sheet.

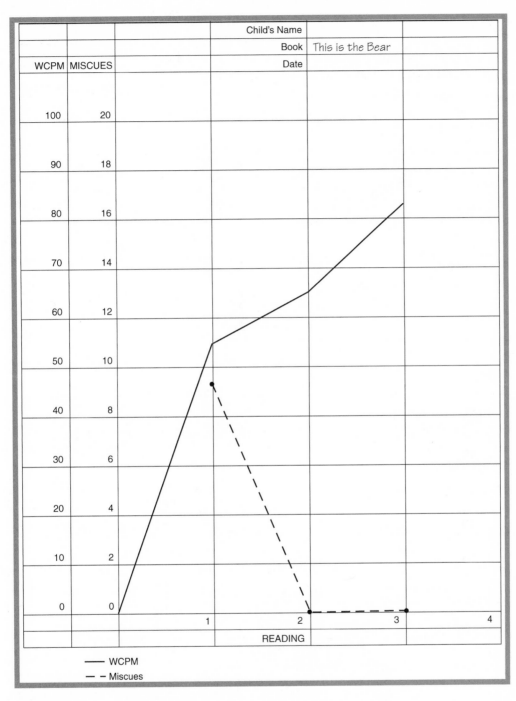

FIGURE 7.6. Example of a completed fluency graph.

FORM 7.2. FLUENCY GRAPH A

CHILD'S NAME _____

BOOK _____

DATE _____

WCPM	MISCUES	1	2	3	4
150	15				
140	14				
130	13				
120	12				
110	11				
100	10				
90	9				
80	8				
70	7				
60	6				
50	5				
40	4				
30	3				
20	2				
10	1				
0	0				

READING

FORM 7.3. FLUENCY GRAPH B

CHILD'S NAME _____

BOOK _____

DATE _____

WCPM	MISCUES					
120	11					
110	10					
100	9					
90	8					
80	7					
70	6					
60	5					
50	4					
40	3					
30	2					
20	1					
10	0					
		1	2	3	4	

READING

The fluency graph includes three components: (1) the number of miscues, (2) the words-correct-per-minute rate, and (3) the number of readings. The number of miscues, which usually decreases with rereadings, and the words-correct-per-minute rate, which usually increases with rereadings, were recorded in either two different colors or two types of lines (see Figure 7.6).

Two blank graphs are provided. On graph A (see Form 7.2) the highest reading rate is 150 words correct per minute, whereas the highest rate on graph B is 120 words correct per minute (see Form 7.3). As the repeated reading session ends, the tutors give the students their graphs to take home, and they leave the record sheet in the tutor's notebook provided by the classroom teacher.

Repeated Reading Book List

Volunteers used a book list developed by the teachers in the district to choose the appropriate texts for their students. This list included the book levels beginning with A as the easiest (Fountas & Pinnell, 1999) and the passage page numbers with the words already counted (see Table 7.2 for a sample). The teachers thought it was important to allow the volunteers to choose the texts, and they wanted to make the selection process easy.

To compile the book list, the teachers met after school to inventory all books available in their book room, list them in alphabetical order, determine the book level, and count out a passage of approximately 100 words, cataloging the starting

TABLE 7.2. Sample of the Repeated Reading Book List

Book title	Level	Start page	End page	No. of words
I Love Mud and Mud Loves Me (Stephens)	D	3	13	106
Shoveling Snow (Cummings)	F	3	16	109
Shoes from Grandpa (Fox)	H	3	10	95
Henry and Mudge (Rylant)	J	14	18	100
Amelia Bedelia Goes Camping (Parish)	K	17	19	101
Cam Jansen and the Mystery of the Babe Ruth Baseball (Adler)	L	12	13	112

Note. Book levels, based on Fountas and Pinnell (1999), increase in difficulty. Level A is "easy."

and ending pages. Although subsequent meetings were arranged to complete the work, almost all of the cataloging was completed during the initial meeting.

Fluency Article

For additional reading, a copy of "Fluency for Everyone: Incorporating Fluency Instruction in the Classroom" (Rasinski, 1989) was provided in the volunteer packet.

Frequently Asked Questions

A list of questions and answers were developed for the volunteers to help them as they planned for instruction (see Table 7.3).

Miscues and Calculating the Words-Correct-per-Minute Rate

Participants were given a "crash course" on keeping running records and noting miscues. They were instructed simply to record the miscues on a blank sheet of paper or a page of matching text. Post-it notes could also be used to mark the miscues right on the text.

The term "miscue" was new to all the tutors; therefore, time was taken to explain what a miscue is and which miscues should be recorded. A miscue, of course, refers to a reader's deviation from written text. Readers use various *cues* (semantic, syntactic, and graphophonic) to read text. A *miscue* does not have the same negative connotation as an error or mistake might.

Table 7.4 was distributed at the meeting so that tutors could follow a format for recording miscues during repeated readings. It was noted that although hesitations, repetitions, missed punctuation, and self-corrections are not counted as miscues in calculating a words-correct-per-minute rate, these could be recorded and then discussed between readings.

The formula for calculating the words-correct-per-minute rate

$$\frac{\text{Number of running words} - \text{number of miscues} \times 60}{\text{Number of seconds}}$$

was reviewed, and participants practiced with a few examples. The examples were then used to practice completing the fluency graph.

Tutors were encouraged to communicate with their classroom teacher and the other class volunteer by writing on sheets provided in the tutor's notebook. This was also the way the teacher would communicate with tutors, because many times teachers were involved in instruction when the volunteers arrived.

TABLE 7.3. Frequently Asked Questions

1. *When should I look for an easier book?*

   Sometimes students struggle on the first reading or fail to improve appropriately. In this case, it may be better to find easier material or talk to the teacher. Consider thinking about choosing a different selection if any of the following applies to your student:

   a. On the first reading the student does not reach 85% accuracy (as a guide, that's more than 1 miscue every 15 words).
   b. On the second reading the student does not reach 90% accuracy (as a guide, that's more than 1 miscue every 10 words).
   c. By the third reading the student has not reached the low target for his on her grade level.
   d. The student is obviously struggling and distressed by a failure to read successfully.

2. *Should I discuss each miscue?*

   Discuss three or four. You might group types of miscues together. It is helpful for students to read the miscued word aloud correctly or to reread the sentence in which it occurs. Keep the time frame of the entire session in mind as well.

3. *Should I get into a discussion about content or comprehension?*

   Comprehension is always the goal of reading. Don't do anything that would move a student away from thinking that it is important. Answer the student's questions about content or clarify something that he or she is unsure about, but lengthy discussions aren't the purpose of fluency practice.

4. *What if my assessment of the student's use of expression and/or punctuation is different from the student's assessment?*

   Keep in mind that a main purpose of the student's self-assessment of expression and punctuation is to raise his or her awareness of these skills as characteristics of good readers. Use this part of the fluency record sheet to discuss briefly what it means to read with expression and with attention to punctuation. You might model these.

5. *What if the rate decreases or miscues increase on the third reading?*

   Consider having the student do a fourth *untimed* reading and emphasize qualitative improvements. In future sessions check to see if there is a dramatic decrease in rate between the first and second readings. If there is, consider leaving the third reading untimed, telling the student to focus on expression. You can also try recording and playing the reading for fun.

TABLE 7.4. Recording Miscues

Use this system when you have a copy of the passage on which to mark.

Mispronunciations and substitutions
   (Write the word the child says.)

Words pronounced for the student
   (Mark a *P* above the word for *pronounced*.)

Omissions (circle) and insertions (^)

Reversals of order
   (~, count as 1 miscue)

Proper nouns
   (Count only the first one mispronounced as a miscue.)

Mark but don't count:
   hesitations
   repetitions
   missed punctuation
   self-corrections

The remainder of the session was devoted to questions, answers, and clarifications. As the meeting concluded, the volunteers were reminded to keep the experience positive and to make any necessary adjustments depending on how the child responded. They were left with the thought that the repeated reading activity for fluency development is process oriented, meaning that the children learn by reviewing and discussing their areas of strength and improvement. The interaction between the child and tutor can improve literacy skills as well as confidence levels. The volunteers left the meeting excited about the program and ready to begin.

Implementation

Within a week of the training session the classroom teachers contacted their volunteers to give them the names of the children with whom they would be working. The teachers invited the tutors to spend time during the first session getting to know the children and establishing trust. It was suggested that the volunteer use a classroom poetry book to share a poem or two during the first session and just talk a bit before starting the repeated reading activity.

During a usual session, the volunteer would enter the classroom and consult the tutor's notebook to gather materials and read any messages from the teacher. Then the volunteer would meet with the students, one at a time, in a predetermined area of the classroom. The repeated reading activity would begin with a prereading discussion, followed by student reading, tutor support, continued repeated readings, record keeping, and the development of the take-home fluency graph. After meeting with his or her assigned children, the volunteer returned the materials and placed the repeated reading record sheets in the tutor's notebook. Many times a note was left for the teacher, highlighting the student's accomplishments. On average, each student session lasted approximately 15–20 minutes.

Frustration, Instructional, and Independent Reading Levels

Before the tutoring program began, appropriate reading levels for fluency development were determined by the classroom teacher for each student participant. However, the responsibility for sustaining the correct reading level for fluency development ultimately became that of the individual tutor. The teacher was always available to assist the tutor, and guidelines were also provided to ensure that the children were reading materials that would allow for success and fluency development.

It was recommended that tutors try to stay close to an instructional level, 90–94% accuracy, when selecting passages for repeated reading. As the students reread at the same level over a period of sessions, their rate will move to that of the independent level, above 94% accuracy. It isn't necessarily bad to work on fluency at an independent level, though; children should have opportunities to listen to themselves read smoothly and effortlessly. The calculation to determine the accuracy is:

$$\frac{\text{Running words} - \text{miscues}}{\text{Running words}} \times 100 = \text{Accuracy percentage}$$

For example, there were 120 words in a passage (running words). The student made nine miscues while reading the passage for the first time. The calculation would be:

$$\frac{120 - 9 = 111}{120} \times 100 = 92.5\%$$

This score is within the instructional level and indicates a good choice for fluency instruction.

Materials for Volunteers

In each participating classroom a tutor's notebook was made from a three-ring binder. The binder contained a large zippered "pencil case" made with a three-hole punch opposite the zippered end. Each pencil case held a calculator, stopwatch, colored pencils, and Post-it notes. The binder contained a section for each student, indicated by a colored tab. Within each student section a sleeve held the book being used by that student at that time. The tutor filed all repeated reading record sheets in each student's section as well. Finally there were sections that held blank record sheets, the leveled book list developed by the classroom teachers, and blank sheets for written communication.

Teachers chose 20–30 book selections from the book room to be stored in a crate next to the tutor's notebook. The levels of these books were labeled (*L, M, N,* etc.), and different books of one level were placed in a resealable bag. Each bag held copies of a list of the book selection titles, with a place for the student's name, so that the tutor could keep track of the titles read. Each book, in turn, held a library pocket and card or Post-it with passage page numbers and the total number of words in the passage. Some teachers included the resource *Matching Books to Readers: Using Leveled Books in Guided Reading, K–3* (Fountas & Pinnell, 1999) in the crate to allow tutors to select titles from the public library that were at the child's reading level but not available at the school.

Mentoring

Volunteer tutors were invited to contact their classroom teachers or the parent coordinator whenever they needed any assistance. This worked out to be a good plan, especially since the parent coordinator was enrolled in a graduate program in reading and was able to answer procedural and literacy questions. The parent coordinator developed two more volunteer meetings for additional learning, based on the needs of the tutors and teachers. As the year progressed, it became apparent that some of the volunteer tutors were greatly interested in further developing the program. These people continue to expand the volunteer program, streamline its management, and perfect the tutor's notebook.

The Thank You Coffee

During the month of May, a celebration was planned. There was much to celebrate and many to thank as the school year came to a close and plans for the following year were already taking shape. One day after school the teachers, administrators, parents, and even some children gathered to honor the fluency tutors. It was agreed that the program was a huge success, thanks to the time commitment of the volunteers—many of whom could hardly wait to begin again in September.

Was It Worth the Time and Effort?

Well, let's see! One volunteer said, "This has gotten a lot of us really excited about what *we* can do to help our children, and it helped me understand one thing the teachers are doing to make our children better readers. With charting progress [on the fluency record sheets and fluency graphs], we can *see* the growth in the children and so can they and their teachers."

At the end of the first year the volunteers filled out a survey; they were very positive in their responses. Seventy percent of the volunteers returned to continue the following year; the total number of tutors increased from 42 the first year to 57 the second year. Indeed, four volunteers enrolled in programs to become teachers or reading specialists, and the district hired the parent coordinator and a volunteer to continue the program. Many neighboring districts asked for information, so that they too might implement a similar program. Was it worth the time and effort? Absolutely!

A PREVIEW OF THE NEXT CHAPTER

Chapter 8 contains a sampling of resources for fluency development. These resources can be easily incorporated into any reading curriculum. In addition, other reference materials are provided.

RESOURCES FOR FLUENCY INSTRUCTION

I n this chapter we invite you to develop a professional bookshelf and resource collection related to fluency. There are many wonderful books and articles that can help you learn about and develop an effective fluency program. Also provided is a sampling of commercial fluency resources available to teachers. These programs give teachers the ability to reinforce and practice fluency skills with ready-made materials. The programs highlighted here can be integrated into content and reading instruction to entice children into fluency practice.

A TEACHER'S BOOKSHELF: PROFESSIONAL RESOURCES FOR FLUENCY INSTRUCTION

No doubt you will want to continue to learn about fluency. Here we provide a brief list of books and articles for your consideration. We have found them to be informative and enlightening.

Allington, R. L. (2006). *What really matters for struggling readers: Designing research-based programs* (2nd ed.). New York: Allyn & Bacon.

Hiebert, E. H. (1998). *Text matters in learning to read* (CIERA Report No. 1-001). Ann Arbor, MI: Center for the Improvement of Early Reading Achievement (www.ciera.org).

Hiebert, E. H. (2004). *The effects of text difficulty on second graders' fluency development.* Retrieved January 8, 2005, from www.textproject.org.

Johns, J. L., & Berglund, R. L. (2002). *Fluency: Questions, answers, evidence-based strategies.* Dubuque, IA: Kendall/Hunt Reading Resources.

Kuhn, M. F., & Stahl, S. A. (2000). *Fluency: A review of developmental and remedial practices* (CIERA Report No. 2-008). Ann Arbor, MI: Center for the Improvement of Early Reading Achievement (www.ciera.org).

Opitz, M. F., Rasinski, T. V., & Bird, L. B. (1998). *Goodbye round robin: Twenty-five effective oral reading strategies.* Portsmouth, NH: Heinemann.

Prescott-Griffin, M. L., & Witherell. N. L. (2004). *Fluency in focus: Comprehension strategies for all young readers.* Portsmouth, NH: Heinemann.

Rasinski, T. V. (2003). *The fluent reader: Oral reading strategies for building word recognition, fluency, and comprehension.* New York: Scholastic.

Rasinski, T. V., & Padak, N. D. (2001). *From phonics to fluency: Effective teaching of decoding and reading fluency in the elementary school.* New York: Longman.

A SAMPLING OF COMMERCIAL MATERIALS FOR FLUENCY INSTRUCTION

Many programs are authored by professors and researchers who are well respected in the field of reading. Programs that support word recognition and comprehension skills, in addition to fluency, are appropriate for children of various ability levels in kindergarten through high school. Story and passage topics are carefully chosen to peak student interest, and some programs even include take-home activities for added practice. Materials in the programs may include CDs for modeling and read-alongs, teacher's manuals, student readers, workbooks, or blackline masters.

The programs summarized below are presented in alphabetical order. Each begins with a brief overview, followed by general directions for implementation. Any additional materials available are noted at the end.

Fluency First

Publisher: Wright Group
Phone: 800-648-2970
Website: www.WrightGroup.com

The Fluency First program, created by Timothy Rasinski, PhD, and Nancy Padak, PhD, is based on the fluency development lesson, a research-based instructional model created by the authors. Fluency First is appropriate for students in kindergarten through third grade; it builds skills in the areas of fluency, word recognition, and comprehension through modeling, coaching, rehearsing, skill and strategy instruction, and performance.

The Fluency First selections include traditional rhymes, songs, jokes, and poetry, with some narrative passages by authors such as Christina Rossetti and E. B. White. Passage selections are reproduced on overhead transparencies and in a student consumable book. The accompanying audio CD allows students to listen to a fluent model, and it also provides support to dysfluent readers. Formal, informal, and student self-assessments are included to measure growth over time.

Steps for Fluency Development

Fluency First is organized to be implemented daily in short sessions. There are six steps: On the first day students (1) listen as the text is introduced, modeled, and (2) read together. The next day the students (3) practice in class, with coaching from the teacher and other students, along with independent work and games to build word recognition and comprehension. Students may also listen to the CD and record a rereading for self-assessment. Children are encouraged to (4) practice at home while (5) building their fluency skills. All five steps are repeated on the third and fourth days with a (6) performance on the fifth day.

All Fluency First materials are available in a complete kit or sold separately. There are no additional materials.

LeapPad, Quantum Pad, and Interactive Library

Publisher: LeapFrog SchoolHouse
Phone: 800-883-7430
Website: www.LeapFrogSchoolHouse.com

The LeapFrog materials were developed as personal learning tools for students in prekindergarten through fifth grades. They include multisensory, interactive technologies with research-based program materials. When using an individual *LeapPad* (younger children) or *Quantum Pad* (older children), students are able to interact with text by touching the book pages with a soft-tipped pen. Students hear the text, are able to get immediate feedback, and repeat the oral reading of text as often as they like. Although the publishers do not advertise that their product promotes fluency development, it appears that it does, in fact, help with fluency by providing fluent models, word recognition, and repetition. The *Read It All* series of books, part of the Interactive Library, provides a "phrase it" feature to support the chunking of text into appropriate phrases.

A wide variety of titles is available in the interactive library, with some selections written by authors such as Marc Brown. A series of titles developed for school use were based on state and national reading standards and include activities for phonemic awareness, decoding, and phrasing. There are also series of leveled selections, cross-curricular topics, and books to be taken home. To develop reading and comprehension, the LeapFrog system includes an audio component to provide unknown words, definitions, chapter previews, think-aloud tips, and author's craft tips.

Steps for Fluency Development

Because this system includes an audio component for immediate feedback, the entire text serves as a fluent model to which students can listen. In addition, the pen feature allows the reading of a whole sentence or just one word. It can even give the sound for one letter in a word. As mentioned, there is a phrasing feature in the *Read It All* series that supports the correct phrasing of text.

Additional Materials

LeapFrog SchoolHouse has a wide variety of materials to consider, including texts in Spanish and materials to support English learning. In addition, free support in grant writing is offered to help schools secure funding to purchase the materials.

Let's Sing about It

Publisher: Mondo
Phone: 800-242-3650
Website: www.mondopub.com

Let's Sing about It is a choral reading program developed to support fluency, oral language skills, print concepts, phonemic awareness, phonics, and (starting in grade 2) comprehension and vocabulary. The readings are appropriate for students in kindergarten through third grade.

The passages for *Let's Sing about It* include rhythmic songs and poems that can be both read and sung. An audiocassette or CD models fluency and includes a music-only selection so that children can sing the words with only the music as a backup. A copy of the text is provided in an enlarged version with a lesson booklet for teachers that includes 4–5 days of activities for each poem/song. Copies of the selections are also available in a format that is easy to reproduce, so that students can have their own copies.

Steps for Fluency Development

A second-grade example included 4 days of lessons with activities for an optional fifth day. Session 1 included building of background knowledge, making personal connections to the topic, choral reading, vocabulary work, and comprehension activities. Sessions for days 2–4 supported fluency development through rereading. Comprehension, vocabulary, and phonics activities were presented. On day 5 optional writing activities were suggested, along with a variety of additional book titles that supported the topic of the poem and could be integrated into the lesson.

Additional Materials

The *Let's Sing about It* program includes big book selections for each of the four grade levels. These big books include a CD providing two versions: one with the words and music and the other with the music only.

QuickReads

Publisher: Pearson Learning Group
Phone: 800-321-3106
Website: www.pearsonlearning.com

The *QuickReads* fluency program was developed and written by Elfrieda Hiebert, PhD. It is based on research she and others conducted on fluency and comprehension. Its systematic procedure is appropriate for students in grades 2–5; it builds skills in the areas of fluency, comprehension, and background knowledge through the reading and rereading of carefully written expository passages covering science and social studies topics.

The *QuickReads* passages, written to be read in about 1 minute's time, include 98% decodable and high-frequency words that students encounter often in reading materials. The rest of the words are content words relating directly to the topic of the passage. These content words are repeated in subsequent passages so that students not only increase their word recognition skills but build vocabulary too.

At each grade level there are 18 *QuickReads* topics divided into nine science and nine social studies selections that match national and state standards. Each topic is fully explored as students build background knowledge and understanding of the topic.

Steps for Fluency Development

To improve fluency, students are given a grade-appropriate passage. The students interact with the passage in three ways. First they participate in the prereading activities of recalling background knowledge of the topic and noting words that may be difficult. They then read the passage at their own rate and fill in a graphic organizer developed to highlight the major ideas of the passage. Next the teacher models a 1-minute reading of the passage aloud to the children while they follow along on their copy. In addition to again highlighting the most important ideas, the teacher explains that the oral reading should help them understand the passage and act as an example for how the reading should sound. Finally, in the third exposure to the passage, the students' goal is to silently read as much as possible in 1 minute's time. They record their rates and complete a comprehension review that consists of open-ended and multiple-choice questions. In addition there are student-guided record sheets to chronicle the reading content and rate, as well as suggestions for supporting and extending the lessons at home.

Support materials for the teacher include optional lesson extensions and assistance for English-language learners. Benchmark passages and analysis instructions are included to assess student growth over time. Further, instructions for modifying the typical lesson routine are included for students who do not meet the benchmark standards.

Read-along CDs, included in the *QuickReads* package, provide fluent models of the passages. Students can use the read-along CD to pace themselves, first, by reading the passage in a minute and, second, by reading the passage at a faster rate as a challenge.

Additional Materials

The *QuickReads* instructional program is also available for students to use independently at the computer in the *QuickReads* Technology Edition. This system includes speech recognition that monitors the student's progress.

The *QuickReads* Technology Edition follows the same structure of three readings, with support in pronunciation and vocabulary obtained by clicking a prompt. The program models the oral reading, prompts the pronunciation of unknown words, records and replays student reading, and records and highlights words read both correctly and incorrectly. Teachers and students can access a record sheet that notes the reading rate, accuracy, reading comprehension, and a list of words students found difficult.

Reading Fluency

Publisher: Jamestown Education McGraw Hill Glencoe
Phone: 800-USA-READ
Website: www.jamestowneducation.com

I [C.B.] developed *Reading Fluency* specifically for use with middle and high school students who struggle with fluency. It is based on research I and others conducted on fluency development and comprehension. This paired oral reading series is appropriate for adolescent readers, with passage selections that sixth through twelfth graders would find interesting. The fiction and nonfiction passages come from popular texts such as *Hatchet* by Gary Paulsen.

The series builds skills in the areas of fluency, vocabulary, and comprehension. It includes 200-word passages of 10 reading levels so that the teacher can match a student's independent level with the reading. The series includes nonconsumable Readers and consumable record sheets.

Steps for Fluency Development

Students improve their oral reading fluency by working in pairs. One student reads aloud from the Reader that includes the passage, and the other student follows along on a copy of the same passage on the record sheet. The listening partner marks errors on the passage record sheet while timing the reading. The oral reading is scored with a words-correct-per-minute rate and the reader's fluency self-assessment. The reader receives immediate feedback after reviewing the first reading with the listening partner. The reader then rereads the same passage, with the listening partner again recording the errors and timing the reading. The oral reading is self-assessed, scored for a second time, and improvement documented.

Additional Materials

Reading Fluency has two additions to supplement the series. First there is an audio CD so that students can listen to fluent models of all the passages. Second, there is a teacher's manual for the series, Teacher Notes, that includes research on fluency, instructional techniques for both the *Reading Fluency* series and other fluency development activities, thoughts on using the passages for placement and assessment, and a fluency reference list.

Read Naturally

Publisher: Read Naturally
Phone: 800-788-4085
Website: www.readnaturally.com

Read Naturally was developed by reading teacher Candyce Ihnot for her master's degree and was initially based on the success of Ihnot's special needs students. Since that time, student success in developing fluency through the use of *Read Naturally* has been documented in eight additional classrooms with both regular and special education students.

Fluency is developed in three steps: (1) modeling, (2) repeated reading, and (3) progress monitoring. The children first listen to a taped rendition of a story read aloud fluently. They then repeatedly read the same selection until they reach a predetermined rate. Finally, they keep records of their progress by graphing their rate. This combination of strategies helps improve the fluency of struggling readers.

Steps for Fluency Development

There are 12 basic steps for implementing *Read Naturally*. Briefly these steps include the following:

1. Students select a story for fluency development at an appropriate reading level.

2. Students predict what the selection might be about.

3. Students time their initial reading for 1 minute to set a baseline.

4. Students graph the number of words read correctly in one minute.

5. Students read along with the audio and the text three times.

6. Students read without the audio support and continue to reread until a predetermined goal is met.

7. Students answer comprehension questions; the teacher tracks the students' responses.

8. The teacher times students individually to ascertain if the preset words-correct-per-minute rate has been met.

9. Students again graph their rates on the same graph as the initial reading to document growth.

10. Students write a retelling or practice word lists.

11. Students select a new story and repeat the process.

12. After completing all stories in one level, the children continue with that same level or move to more difficult material.

Additional Materials

The *Read Naturally* leveled stories include a phonics, multicultural, and Spanish series in addition to the sequenced edition. There is also a wide selection of materials available from *Read Naturally*, such as timers, cassette players, and headphones. A full day training seminar video is offered as well.

Two Voices: A Read-Along Series

Publisher: Options Publishing
Phone: 800-782-7300
Website: www.optionspublishing.com

The *Two Voices* book selections provide support for parents who want to assist their children in literacy learning at home. The books are organized to allow a parent–

child pair to both read along and read aloud. Appropriate for children in kindergarten through second grade, this book series builds fluency, word recognition, and comprehension.

The *Two Voices* collection includes short stories and poems with text that includes rhythm, rhyme, and repeated words and phrases supported by colorful illustrations. The text itself is color-coded to help readers determine who should read; the adult reads the purple lines, the child reads the red lines, and together both the adult and child read the green lines. This system allows for choral reading, partner reading, and, when necessary, echo reading. Rereadings of the selections build fluency and confidence. Instructions and ideas for parents are listed at the beginning of each book.

There are four thematic titles for each grade level; the topics are appropriate for the interests of children at each grade level and include a mixture of narrative and expository selections, with a rebus design in the kindergarten texts. An audio CD is included to model fluent reading.

Steps for Fluency Development

To begin, the *Two Voices* thematic book is introduced at school. Then, in a backpack provided by the publisher, the book and CD are taken home for rereading. A note to the adult reader is included in the book to provide some background on the book selection and to encourage reading daily for fun.

The instructions to the adult reader in one book include ideas on how to introduce the title, conduct a picture walk, and share a vocabulary strategy, along with notes on print awareness, supports for a postreading discussion, and information on the importance of rereading. The instructions are easy to read and follow. There were no additional support materials available for *Two Voices: A Read-Along Series.*

AND ON TO THE FINAL CHAPTER . . .

Now that you have added fluency development to your expertise, share it with others! Chapter 9 highlights fluency for staff development as well as helping you to consider implementation strategies in the classroom.

CHAPTER 9

FLUENCY AS A FOCUS FOR TEACHER LEARNING

Sometimes the best learning takes place by accident. When we and others were invited to work in a multiethnic district to improve reading instruction, we embarked on a collaborative investigation to see if instruction for fluency could improve student performance. Along the way, the process of developing this program resulted in a staff development program and volunteer program, many aspects of which we described in earlier chapters.

The project, called Everybody Reads, had three goals:

1. To develop classroom-tested models for building reading fluency in grades K–3.

2. To design a tutoring model for fluency to be delivered by volunteer tutors.

3. To increase the engagement of teachers in planning and carrying out their own staff development.

In this chapter, we describe the ways in which fluency instruction had a three-fold outcome for the district: (1) It improved the fluency of the elementary students in the project, (2) provided an excellent focus for the development of an effective volunteer tutoring program, and (3) provided a point of departure for teacher staff development that led teacher inquiry far beyond this single instructional issue.

WHY WAS FLUENCY THE TARGET FOR STUDENTS?

As we clearly described in Chapters 1 and 2, the ability to read fluently (i.e., at a good rate, with good accuracy, and with proper intonation and phrasing) is highly correlated with many measures of reading competence (Kuhn & Stahl, 2000; Strecker et al., 1998). For the reader, fluency requires good decoding skills, the strategies to orchestrate these in reading real text, and comprehension to monitor if what is being read aloud sounds like language. For the teacher, listening to students read and charting their development in fluency are also ways to measure the effect of instruction and to collect input for further instructional planning. Unlike most standardized measures, which only show large changes in behavior, fluency measurement is sensitive to small increments of improvement (Shinn, 1989). And, unlike standardized measures, the practice involved in the reading of a fluency measurement passage can also help students' reading. Fluency is not only a good *measure* of reading performance, but working toward fluency is also a good *treatment* for reading difficulties. Requiring students to do a lot of reading at an appropriate level, with a teacher, tutor, or peer supporting them and helping them to self-monitor, is a good way for students to practice their way to competence (Rasinski, Padak, Linek, & Sturtevant, 1994).

WHY IS FLUENCY A GOOD FOCUS FOR STAFF DEVELOPMENT?

With regard to staff development, several issues are embedded in fluency work that are critical to classroom instruction and address the empirical questions of educators. Teachers who are concerned with their students' fluency need to ask and answer several questions that have ramifications far beyond the realm of fluency instruction:

➤ How do I know what my class can handle?

➤ What materials do I need so that everybody can read?

➤ How do I build activities into the day so that every student reads every day on an appropriate level?

➤ How do I measure and show growth?

These are rich questions that grow out of investigations of fluency but have much further-reaching effects on classroom instruction.

WHAT WAS THE WORKING MODEL FOR THE STAFF DEVELOPMENT COMPONENT?

Two primary teachers from each of the district's 12 public schools and 1 participating private school worked for 2 years, after school and during the summer, to design the project, which was supported administratively by the district's director of reading. University faculty led monthly meetings and worked with three master teachers/facilitators. Over 300 students were involved in the project, with four targeted students from each classroom also receiving extra individual help.

Teachers came together to ask questions about fluency and to receive resources, articles and books, videos, and ideas from the facilitators. After each meeting, teachers tried strategies, read articles, and brought back ideas to the group. Each teacher who volunteered received either a stipend or district credit for pay-scale advancement. Participants needed to commit to trying out strategies and reporting back to the group and their principals. They decided on the goal of developing a set of classroom activities that would *not* lay another bit of curriculum on the day but would "put a fluency spin" on all the instruction they did (Rasinski & Zutell, 1990). This fluency spin would increase the incidence of the following instructional activities:

➢ More modeling of fluent reading.

➢ More support during reading provided by teacher, tutor, or partner.

➢ More repeated reading practice in various forms.

➢ More emphasis of good phrasing and expression in reading.

➢ More careful matching of students and texts.

Just as an example, teachers using poetry would be sure to read aloud the poem under study several times, or have students listen to a recorded version of the poem so that they would be exposed to good models. The class would do choral reading or support reading, with the teacher's voice fading in and out as the students became confident readers. After the readings of the poem, there might be a mini-lesson on punctuation and phrasing, perhaps having students draw pause marks or stop signs as reminders to stop, and underlining phrases where the words went together. Then students would read to each other, in partner sets, or with take-home poems for further practice. The materials were now easy for the students to read independently, which made it easy for them to share their new skills with family members.

Teachers worked during the year to develop a handbook of resources (a favorite was Opitz et al., 1998; also Stahl & Kuhn, 2002) and exemplary videos. The teachers, district, and university staff created transparencies, handouts, and PowerPoint presentations to illustrate the issues that teachers decided were important and could be shared with other teachers in school mini-workshops (available for downloading at www.illinoisreads.com). The handbooks were organized around these topics, which reflected the inquiry questions they pursued over the course of the year:

1. What is fluency and why is it important?

2. How do I assess and observe my students and make a fluency snapshot of my whole class?

3. How do I match students with materials?

4. What are some methods for increasing fluency in the classroom?

5. What is an individual tutorial model for increasing fluency?

For example, you can't do fluency work if you don't know your students' reading levels and what materials match their needs. For assessment, teachers decided to use the classroom fluency snapshot (Blachowicz et al., 2001) in the fall, winter, and spring to provide a quick overview of each classroom as a "thermometer" of progress (see Chapter 3 for examples). Once it was clear that there was a range of reading levels in each class, the teachers asked for sessions on material leveling and then organized their own work sessions on leveling. They developed and shared ways to store and share materials in schools and created a video for others on organizing materials. So the seemingly simple concept of fluency led to a significant amount of teacher inquiry and sharing.

WHAT WERE THE RESULTS?

Student Growth in Fluency

The primary goal, of course, was the improvement of student fluency. Second grade was the target group for this project because that is the grade when students must develop fluency, beyond the initial stages of decoding, to make the next leap in reading improvement. Looking at three second-grade classrooms participating in the project as compared to their contrast classrooms from the same grade and school that did not participate, an analysis of covariance, which controlled for pre-test level, was used to examine the fluency gains in words correct per minute. The gains in the project classrooms were statistically superior to those of their matched grade level and school classrooms ($F = 2.472$; $p < .038$).

Individual Improvement

There was also a statistically significant effect for those receiving the volunteer fluency training we detailed in Chapter 7: t-tests were conducted to compare pairs, and tutored students experienced significantly greater gains in fluency over the course of the 6-month trial ($t = -2.86$, $p < .010$).

Teacher Growth

As well as growth in student fluency, we saw significant teacher growth from our work in fluency. All 25 participating teachers filled out a postprogram evaluation on their learning, using a 5-point Likert scale and anecdotal comments. On the scale items, based on a 5-point scale, the averages were:

> Increased my knowledge and expertise.   5.0

> Provided new techniques and strategies.   4.9

> I intend to continue using these strategies after the project.   4.8

> Encouraged me to undertake further professional development.   4.8

With regard to disseminating the program, 17 of the 25 teachers said, in anecdotal comments, that they had used the new assessment strategies to share information with parents during conferences. All of the teachers reported sharing materials and strategies with others in their school.

As a further test of the teachers' commitment to supporting and disseminating the project, participating teachers volunteered to offer an in-district course on fluency, using the created materials. Seventy-three new district teachers signed up for the course, which was then offered on four different school sites. This course has continued into year 4 of the project, 2 years after university and state support ended. The local press and media have shared the project with the community in print and video, and the Illinois State Board of Education now makes a complete set of project materials available on its website. Teachers have also presented the project at local and state reading councils and are going to other schools and districts to disseminate the model.

FLUENCY AND STAFF DEVELOPMENT

Our work in district professional development shows how a simple concept such as fluency development can inspire deep and meaningful inquiry by classroom teachers and volunteers, who then take charge of the direction and development of further investigation. Project teachers have decided how to continue and refine the project. Several have been stimulated to undertake graduate study because of the incentive provided by the project. Some first-grade teachers, dissatisfied with fluency as a key for beginning reading improvement, have started a project called "Rethinking First-Grade Instruction" that looks at the precursors to fluency instruction. In addition, committed volunteers are modifying the volunteer handbook with their own ideas.

Working with fluency in the classroom is both a good learning experience for you and your students, and a source of shared vocabulary and focus for school staff growth. With improved fluency, the confidence level of students increases. With this confidence students spend more time reading, which in turn allows for additional practice and further improvement. Students experience success, become more engaged, and know they are doing well. We have even observed some children express a preference to read over other activities, after experiencing an improvement in fluency. One child said, "You know, reading isn't boring any more." And isn't this what we want—children who read fluently, understand, and are able to derive great pleasure from the reading experience?

FLUENCY AND THE READING CURRICULUM

If you already have your literacy program established, it's still easy to find the time for fluency. Here are 10 ideas:

➤ After guided reading, send students off in pairs to reread a portion of the text to each other.

➤ Include fluency practice in sustained silent reading (SSR). Create book bags full of texts read during guided reading. During SSR time, students select a 100–300 word passage from their book bag to reread in addition to their regular SSR selection.

➤ Once a week put aside 20 minutes for the fluency development lesson (see Chapter 5)—it takes a relatively short time and will benefit many!

➤ Add a poem of the week to the start of the day; students read the poem chorally each day of the week.

➤ Provide a tape recorder and cassettes for the recording of fluent reading. During free time children can practice reading aloud until they are fluent. The reading is then recorded. The reader and the book are introduced, and the selection is read into the tape recorder. The book is left at the listening center for others to listen to and follow along with their book.

➤ Fluency practice is perfect for homework. Send independent-level passages home for rereading. One teacher encouraged students to call their grandparents, aunts, uncles, and cousins and read to them. These students then kept a log of the date, what they read, and to whom they read. The children enjoyed keeping track, and family members appreciated staying in touch.

➤ Read to your buddy! In many schools a primary class is "buddied" with an upper elementary class for activities. Reading fits in perfectly with this format. Both younger and older students choose a book to read to their buddy. The fluency work comes in rereading the book for practice before it is read to the buddy.

➤ Preparation for author's chair can include fluency in the form of rereading. In this way the oral reading of the student's writing is fluent.

➤ Set up a listening center. Books and tapes are available through book clubs, public libraries, and used-book sellers. Children can listen to fluent models and follow along in the book.

➤ Invite a "royal reader" to the class once or twice a week. Royal readers include parents, staff, administration, or community members who visit the classroom to model fluent oral reading for individuals or small groups of students. Book selections can be made by the children or by the royal reader.

CLOSING THOUGHTS

In this book we have shared the ideas and resources we have gathered during more than 10 years of working on fluency instruction in the schools. We hope these ideas and resources provide you with a smooth entrance into the world of fluency instruction. Our charts, materials, and strategies have been field tested so that you will have the support you need to structure effective instruction.

We know you are excited to begin, but you may want to start small and build your expertise. We suggest administering a classroom fluency snapshot in September. Use this information to target three to five students for intensive fluency instruction while you integrate different fluency lessons, such as poetry performances, into your reading curriculum to benefit all students. This approach gives you a chance to practice without becoming overwhelmed. Repeat the CFS in January and reevaluate your focus students. At this time you might be ready to invite volunteers to work with students or perhaps train your students to manage their own repeated reading sessions.

So, be bold and get started. Try to "put a fluency spin" on everything you do in your classroom, every day. Remember to . . .

➤ Provide a wide range of materials so that your students can work on appropriate levels.

➤ Make time for students to share what they read—read an exciting part, a funny part, an interesting part, a beautifully written part. Consider daily oral fluency sharing.

➤ Find every chance you can for students to do purposeful oral reading—reading to answer a question, prove a point, clarify, or raise a question.

➤ Focus on more than pace; read for expressiveness and for sharing.

➤ Help classroom volunteers become aware of fluency goals so that they can help students achieve them.

➤ Remember the power of modeling—you are a model, as are the other good readers you invite into your classroom to engage your students in listening to good reading.

We hope you have enjoyed being *our* partner in fluency. Keep the spin going!

REFERENCES

Adler, D. (1998). *Cam Jansen and the mystery of the Babe Ruth baseball*. London: Puffin.

Allington, R. L. (1983). Fluency: The neglected reading goal. *The Reading Teacher, 36,* 556–561.

Allington, R. L. (2006). *What really matters for struggling readers: Designing research-based programs* (2nd ed.). New York: Allyn & Bacon.

Barr, R., Blachowicz, C. L. Z., Katz, C., & Kaufman, B. (2002). *Reading diagnosis for teachers: An instructional approach*. Boston: Allyn & Bacon.

Bear, D. R. (1991). "Learning to fasten the seat of my union suit without looking around": The synchrony of literacy development. *Theory into Practice, 30,* 149–157.

Bear, D. R., Invernizzi, M., Templeton, S., & Johnston, F. (2004). *Words their way*. Upper Saddle River, NJ: Pearson Merrill Prentice Hall.

Betts, E. A. (1954). *Foundations of reading instruction* (rev. ed.). New York: American Book.

Blachowicz, C. L. Z., Fisher, P., Obrochta, C., Massarelli, J., Moskal, M. K., & Jones, S. (2000). *Everybody Reads fluency development program*. Springfield, IL: Illinois State Board of Education.

Blachowicz, C. L. Z., Moskal, M. K., Massarelli, J. R., Obrochta, C. M., Fogelberg, E., & Fisher, P. (2006). "Everybody reads": Fluency as a focus for staff development. In T. Rasinski, C. Blachowicz, & K. Lems (Eds.), *Fluency instruction: Research-based best practices* (pp. 141–154). New York: Guilford Press.

Blachowicz, C. L. Z., & Obrochta, C. (2005). Vocabulary visits: Virtual field trips for content vocabulary development. *The Reading Teacher, 59,* 262–268.

Blachowicz, C. L. Z., Sullivan, D., & Cieply, C. (2001). Fluency snapshots: A quick screening tool for your classroom. *Reading Psychology, 22,* 95–109.

Blume, J. (1991). *Tales of a fourth grade nothing.* New York: Laurel Leaf.

Breznitz, Z. (1987). Increasing first graders' reading accuracy and comprehension by accelerating their reading rates. *Journal of Educational Psychology, 79,* 236–242.

Briggs, C., & Forbes, S. (2002). Phrasing in fluent reading: Process and product. *Journal of Reading Recovery, 1,* 1–19.

Buckley, J., Jr. (2003). *The world of baseball.* New York: DK Publishing.

Caine, R. N., & Caine, G. (1991). *Making connections: Teaching and the human brain.* Alexandria, VA: Association for Supervision and Curriculum Development.

Chomsky, C. (1976). After decoding: What? *Language Arts, 53,* 288–296, 314.

Clark, C. H. (1995). Teaching students about reading: A fluency example. *Reading Horizons, 35,* 250–266.

Clay, M. M. (2002). *An observation survey.* Portsmouth, ME: Heinemann.

Covey, S. R. (1989). *The seven habits of highly effective people: Restoring the character ethic.* New York: Simon & Schuster.

Cummings, P. (1994). *Shoveling snow.* New York: Scholastic.

Dewey, J. (1944). *Democracy in education: An introduction to the philosophy of education.* New York: Free Press. (Original work published 1916)

Dickinson, D. R., & Smith, M. W. (1994). Long-term effects of preschool teachers' book readings on low income children's vocabulary and story comprehension. *Reading Research Quarterly, 29,* 104–122.

Dorn, L., French, C., & Jones, T. (1998). *An apprenticeship in literacy: Transitions across reading and writing.* York, ME: Stenhouse.

Dowhower, S. L. (1986). The effect of repeated reading on selected second graders' oral reading fluency and comprehension (doctoral dissertation, the University of Wisconsin–Madison). *Dissertation Abstracts International, 47-07A,* 2523.

Dowhower, S. L. (1987). Effects of repeated reading on second-grade transitional readers' fluency and comprehension. *Reading Research Quarterly, 22,* 389–406.

Dowhower, S. L. (1989). Repeated reading: Research into practice. *The Reading Teacher, 43,* 502–507.

Dowhower, S. L. (1991). Speaking of prosody: Fluency's unattended bedfellow. *Theory into Practice, 30,* 165–175.

Eldredge, J. L. (1990). Increasing the performance of poor readers in the third grade with a group-assisted strategy. *Journal of Educational Research, 84,* 69–77.

Fleischman, P. (1985). *I am phoenix: Poems for two voices.* New York: HarperCollins.

Fleischman, P. (1988). *Joyful noise: Poems for two voices.* New York: HarperCollins.

Fleischman, P. (2000). *Big talk: Poems for four voices.* Cambridge, MA: Candlewick.

Forman, E. A., & Cazden, C. B. (1994). Exploring Vygotskian perspectives in education: The cognitive value of peer interaction. In R. B. Ruddell, M. R. Ruddell, & H. Singer (Eds.), *Theoretical models and processes of reading* (4th ed., pp. 155–178). Newark, DE: International Reading Association.

Fountas, I., & Pinnell, G. S. (1999). *Matching books to readers: Using leveled books in guided reading, K–3.* Portsmouth, NH: Heinemann.

Fox, M. (1990). *Shoes from grandpa.* London: Orchard Books.

Guiberson, B. Z. (1996). *Into the sea.* New York: Holt.

Guszak, F. J. (1992). *Reading for students with special needs.* Dubuque, IA: Kendall/Hunt Reading Resources.

Herman, P. A. (1985). The effect of repeated readings on reading rate, speech pauses, and word recognition accuracy. *Reading Research Quarterly, 20*, 553–565.

Hiebert, E. H. (1998). *Text matters in learning to read* (CIERA Report No. 1-001). Ann Arbor, MI: Center for the Improvement of Early Reading Achievement (www.ciera.org).

Hiebert, E. H. (2004). *The effects of text difficulty on second graders' fluency development.* Retrieved January 8, 2005, from www.textproject.org.

Hiebert, E. H., & Fisher, C. W. (2002, April). *Text matters in developing reading fluency.* Paper presented at the meeting of the International Reading Association, San Francisco, CA.

Jamestown Education McGraw Hill Glencoe. (2004). *Helping all readers become better readers* [Brochure]. Columbus, OH: Author.

Johns, J. L. (2005). *Basic reading inventory.* Dubuque, IA: Kendall/Hunt Reading Resources.

Johns, J. L., & Berglund, R. L. (2002). *Fluency: Questions, answers, evidence-based strategies.* Dubuque, IA: Kendall/Hunt Reading Resources.

Johnson, G. M. (1998). Principles of instruction for at-risk learners. *Preventing School Failure, 42*, 167–174.

Johnson, L., Graham, S., & Harris, K. R. (1997). The effects of goal setting and self-instruction on learning a reading comprehension strategy: A study of students with learning disabilities. *Journal of Learning Disabilities, 30*, 80–90.

King-Sears, M. E., & Carpenter, S. L. (1997). *Teaching self-management to elementary students with developmental disabilities.* Washington, DC: American Association on Mental Retardation.

Koskinen, P. S., & Blum, I. H. (1986). Paired repeated reading: A classroom strategy for developing fluent reading. *The Reading Teacher, 40*, 70–75.

Kuhn, M. R., & Stahl, S. A. (2000). *Fluency: A review of developmental and remedial practices* (CIERA Report No. 2-008). Ann Arbor, MI: Center for the Improvement of Early Reading Achievement.

LaBerge, D., & Samuels, S. J. (1974). Toward a theory of automatic processing in reading. *Cognitive Psychology, 6*, 193–323.

LeapFrog SchoolHouse. (2004). *Leapfrog schoolhouse: Unlocking learning potential* [Brochure]. Emeryville, CA: Author.

Lipson, M. Y., & Lang, L. B. (1991). Not as easy as it seems: Some unresolved questions about fluency. *Theory into Practice, 30*, 218–227.

Martin, B., Jr. (1983). *Brown bear, brown bear, what do you see?* New York: Holt.

Martinez, M., Roser, N. L., & Strecker, S. (1998/1999). "I never thought I could be a star": A Readers' Theatre ticket to fluency. *The Reading Teacher, 52*, 326–334.

McDougall, D., & Brady, M. P. (1998). Initiating and fading self-management interventions to increase math fluency in general education classes. *Exceptional Children, 64*, 151–166.

Milne, A. A. (1952). *When we were very young.* New York: Yearling.

Mondo Publishing. (2004). *Hiccup! Hiccup! Shared reading songs, poems, and drama* [Brochure]. New York: Author.

Mondo Publishing. (2004). *Let's sing about it* [Brochure]. New York: Author.

Moskal, M. K. (2002). *The effect of repeated reading on oral reading fluency when implemented by novice peer partners through collaborative student self-managed learning.* Unpublished doctoral dissertation, National-Louis University, Evanston, IL.

Moskal, M. K. (2005, May). *The fluency experts: Students supporting their own fluency develop-*

ment. Paper presented at the annual meeting of the International Reading Association, San Antonio, TX.

Nathan, R. G., & Stanovich, K. E. (1991). The causes and consequences of differences in reading fluency. *Theory into Practice, 30,* 176–184.

Opitz, M. F., Rasinski, T. V., & Bird, L. B. (1998). *Goodbye round robin reading: Twenty-five effective oral reading strategies.* Portsmouth, NH: Heinemann.

Options Publishing. (2004). *Two voices: A read-along series. A parent-involvement program to encourage parent–child interaction for beginning readers* [Brochure]. Merrimack, NH: Author.

Parish, P. (1986). *Amelia Bedelia goes camping.* New York: Avon Books.

Park, B. (2001). *Junie B. June is a graduation girl.* New York: Random House.

Pearson Learning Group. (2004). *Guide your students to reading success with QuickReads: A research-based fluency program. Sampler* [Brochure]. Lebanon, IN: Author.

Perkinson, H. J. (1976). *Two hundred years of American educational thought.* New York: Longman.

Pinnell, G. S., Pikulski, J. J., Wixson, K. K., Campbell, J. R., Gough, P. B., & Beatty, A. S. (1995). *Listening to children read aloud* (National Center for Education Statistics Report No. 23-FR-04). Washington, DC: U.S. Department of Education, National Center for Education Statistics.

Prescott-Griffin, M. L., & Witherell. N. L. (2004). *Fluency in focus: Comprehension strategies for all young readers.* Portsmouth, NH: Heinemann.

Rasinski, T. V. (1989). Fluency for everyone: Incorporating fluency instruction in the classroom. *The Reading Teacher, 42,* 690–693.

Rasinski, T. V. (2003). *The fluent reader: Oral reading strategies for building word recognition, fluency, and comprehension.* New York: Scholastic.

Rasinski, T. V. (2004). Creating fluent readers. *Educational Leadership, 61*(8), 46–51.

Rasinski, T. V., & Padak, N. D. (2001). *From phonics to fluency: Effective teaching of decoding and reading fluency in the elementary school.* New York: Longman.

Rasinski, T. V., Padak, N., Linek, W., & Sturtevant, E. (1994). Effects of fluency development in urban second-grade readers. *Journal of Educational Research, 87,* 158–165.

Rasinski, T. V., & Zutell, J. B. (1990). Making a place for fluency instruction in the regular reading curriculum. *Reading Research and Instruction, 29,* 85–91.

Read Naturally. (2002). *Read naturally: Rationale and research* [Brochure]. St. Paul, MN: Author.

Rogoff, B. (1990). *Apprenticeship in thinking: Cognitive development in social context.* New York: Oxford University Press.

Rylant, C. (1990). *Henry and Mudge: The first book of their adventures.* New York: Aladdin Paperbacks.

Samuels, S. J. (1979). The method of repeated readings. *The Reading Teacher, 32,* 403–408.

Samuels, S. J. (1994). Word recognition. In R. D. Ruddell, M. R. Ruddell, & H. Singer (Eds.), *Theoretical models and processes of reading* (4th ed., pp. 359–380). Newark, DE: International Reading Association.

Schreiber, P. A. (1980). On the acquisition of reading fluency. *Journal of Reading Behavior, 12,* 177–186.

Shinn, M. R. (1989). *Curriculum-based measurement: Assessing special children.* New York: Guilford Press.

Simmons, D. C., & Kame'enui, E. J. (1999). *Curriculum maps: Instruction to achieve instructional priorities in beginning reading kindergarten–grade three*. Eugene, OR: University of Oregon, Institute for the Development of Educational Achievement.

Stahl, S. A. (1996). Reading fluency: The neglected goal. *Illinois Reading Council Journal, 24*(4), 85–91.

Stahl, S., & Kuhn, M. R. (2002). Making it sound like language: Developing fluency. *The Reading Teacher, 55*, 582–584.

Stanovich, K. (2000). *Progress in understanding reading: Scientific foundations and new frontiers*. New York: Guilford Press.

Stephens, V. (1994). *I love mud and mud loves me*. New York: Scholastic.

Stevens, J., & Crummel, S. S. (1999). *Cook-a-doodle-doo!* San Diego, CA: Harcourt Brace.

Strecker, S. K., Roser, N. L., & Martinez, M. G. (1998). Toward understanding oral reading fluency. In T. Shanahan & F. V. Rodriquez-Brown (Eds.), *National reading conference yearbook* (Vol. 47, pp. 295–310). Chicago: National Reading Conference.

Wolf, S. A. (1994). Learning to act/acting to learn: Children as actors, critics, and characters in classroom theater. *Research in the Teaching of English, 28*(1), 7–44.

Wright Group. (2005). *Fluency first: Daily routines to develop reading fluency. Teacher sampler* [Brochure]. DeSoto, TX: Author.

Zutell, J., & Rasinski, T. V. (1991). Training teachers to attend to their students' oral reading fluency. *Theory into Practice, 30*, 211–217.

INDEX

"f" following a page number indicates a figure or a form; "t" following a page number indicates a table.